CONGRESS AND LOBBIES

CONGRESS AND LOBBIES

IMAGE
and REALITY

by ANDREW M. SCOTT
MARGARET A. HUNT

LUX
LIBERTAS

The University of
North Carolina Press   Chapel Hill

Preface

The research described in this volume was undertaken in order to shed light on the relationship of interest groups to Congressional decision-making. Most of the writing on this question has centered on the activities of interest groups despite the fact that it is the congressman who must finally cast his vote in committee or on the House floor, not the interest group representative. Interest groups can have a direct influence on Congressional decision-making only insofar as they have an effect on individual congressmen. For that reason, the authors have chosen to concentrate their attention on the way that congressmen view interest groups.

The findings are based on a series of interviews with congressmen during the second session of the 86th Congress. Respondents for the study were randomly selected from the entire membership of the House of Representatives, excluding those congressmen who constituted the House leadership. For purposes of this study, this leadership consisted of the Speaker of the House, the floor leader and whips of each party, the chairman and ranking minority member of each of the twenty standing committees, and the ranking Democratic and Republican House members of the following joint committees: Atomic Energy, Defense Production, Economic, Internal Revenue Taxation. Because there was some overlapping of official positions the leadership consisted of forty-nine congressmen. There were 437 seats and 6 vacancies in the second session of the 86th Congress, so the actual membership of the House consisted of 431 incumbents. When the 49 House leaders were excluded, the sample universe included 382 congressmen.

The names of these 382 congressmen were group alphabetically, numbered, and a sample of 40 was chosen using a table of random numbers. In addition, ten replacements were selected by random numbers, the replacements to be used only when a respondent in the sample of forty was not available for interviewing. Three respondents were used for a pre-test, two of whose names came from the list of replacements. The third was the congressman from the interviewer's home district.

Of the forty potential respondents, three refused to be interviewed. Interviews could not be arranged with seven others despite efforts extending from six to ten weeks, and the names of four respondents were drawn from the replacement list to substitute for them. Thirty-four of the forty interviews projected were completed before the end of the session, which terminated the interviewing. The sample represents approximately 9 per cent of the universe.

Three criteria were used to test the representatives of the sample: party affiliation, population density of the district represented, and length of continuous service in the House. Of the 382 congressmen, 253 (66 per cent) were Democrats, and of the 34 respondents, 22 (65 per cent) were Democrats. The test of the sample by population density revealed that districts containing at least one medium-sized city were slightly over-represented in the sample and rural areas were slightly under-represented. Of the 382 congressmen, 132 (35 per cent) represented districts with fewer than 65 persons per square mile, but 10 of the 34 congressmen in the sample (29 per cent) represented such districts. Of the congressmen in the universe, 124 (32 per cent) represented districts with 65 to 650 persons per square mile, while 14 (42 per cent) of the sample represented such districts. Finally, 126 (33 per cent) of the congressmen in the universe represented districts with 650 or more persons per square mile, and in the sample, 10 (29 per cent) represented such districts.[1]

In testing the sample by length of Congressional service, congressmen were categorized by the date on which they began their first full term in the House of Representatives. In the category of "low seniority" were placed congressmen who began their first full term of office on January 3, 1959; "medium seniority" congressmen were those in their second, third, or fourth continuous term in the House; and "high seniority" congressmen were those who were serving their fifth or more full term. Of the 382 congressmen in the universe, 92 (24 per cent) had low seniority, 144 (38 per cent) had medium seniority, and 146 (38 per cent) had high seniority. In the sample, 9 congressmen (27 per cent) had low seniority, 11 (32 per cent) had medium seniority, and 14 (41 per cent) had high seniority. These three tests suggest that the sample offers an adequate representation of the universe from which it was drawn.

Each respondent was asked questions dealing with his

---

1. Data were taken from U.S. Bureau of the Census, *Congressional District Data Book: Districts of the 87th Congress*, pp. 4-73. The figures in this volume were drawn from the 1960 census, but the district boundaries were those based on the 1950 census.

perception of interest group activity in a field in which he specialized and in a field in which he did not specialize. The questions were identical in both cases. In addition, he was asked questions designed to reveal his perceptions of interest group activity in general and his attitudes toward that activity. Most of the interviews were approximately thirty minutes in length while, at the extremes, they ran from fifteen minutes to three hours. A copy of the interview schedule appears as an appendix.

Many of the questions used were open-ended, which creates problems for the analyst, but their use seemed indicated in an exploratory study. Analysis of material gained from open-ended questions places a heavy responsibility on the researcher if distortion is to be avoided, and the authors have sought to remain alert to this responsibility. They have also called the attention of the reader to the use of "small numbers" from time to time when the sample was subdivided and there were but a few cases in each category. When dealing with a small "N" they have stated their conclusions tentatively.

The leadership of the House of Representatives is not examined in the study despite the importance of this leadership in the functioning of the House. The reason for the omission is a practical one—the difficulty of obtaining enough interviews with these extremely busy men to justify the use of quantitative techniques of analysis. A full understanding of the subject of this inquiry will require a supplementary study of the perceptions of House leaders of interest group activities.

The picture of interest group influence that emerges from the interviews is sometimes out of keeping with customary beliefs concerning interest group potency. A number of our students have sought to explain the discrepancy by arguing that congressmen dared not acknowledge the extent to which they were under the influence of interest groups and hence, deliberately or otherwise, misled the authors. The authors, however, have not the slightest fear that they were the victims of wholesale deception. Many researchers have found congressmen unusually articulate and candid, and our experience was no exception.

The project was planned jointly by the authors and was financed by a grant from the Faculty Research Council of The University of North Carolina at Chapel Hill and a grant from the Faculty Research Council of The University of North Carolina at Greensboro. The interviewing was done by Margaret Hunt, and the manuscript was prepared jointly.

The Honorable Carl T. Durham, former congressman from the 6th District of North Carolina was generous in allowing the use of his office as headquarters while the field work was under way. Mrs. Margaret Graves, Mrs. Bill Williams, and Mrs. Sue Brienza—all members of Congressman Durham's staff—were of valuable assistance in many ways. Thanks also go to Mrs. Geraldine Foster for valuable editorial assistance during the preparation of this manuscript.

Finally, thanks must go to the respondents, the congressmen who gave generously of time they could not easily spare.

Contents

Tables

CONGRESS AND LOBBIES

Chapter 1

Congress and Interest Groups

Folklore and Fact

The members of a society normally accept certain stereotyped notions about the nature and functioning of their society, including the political system. Some of these notions will have been incorporated into the formal ideology of the community, while others are found in its informal ideology. Both idea systems are likely to have a strong hold on the minds of the citizenry, and neither has necessarily more than a nodding acquaintance with the truth. The elements in one ideology need not be wholly congruent with the elements in the other. Most Americans, for example, might agree that the American government is second to

none and also agree that "politics is a dirty business and
politicians are usually crooks." By and large, the more flattering elements will be incorporated in the formal ideology,
while the less flattering elements will be included in the informal.

One such element in the informal ideology of Americans maintains that the Congress of the United States is
dominated by lobbies and pressure groups. The man in the
street, the lady of the house, and the college freshman "know"
this to be true, although they may be innocent of factual
support for this conviction. They "know" it for the same
reason that they know a variety of other things—the knowledge has been enshrined in the folk culture. Although not
among the great truths that Americans hold to be self-evi-
dent, this belief nevertheless has considerable standing. It
is treated as an axiom rather than a hypothesis, which means
that when its adherents proclaim it they do not expect argument.

It is intriguing that Americans find it so easy and attractive to believe that Congress is a tool of vested interests.
This view of Congress has not always been dominant in the
United States, and no doubt its origins and emergence could
be traced historically. It is associated with the low esteem
that most Americans accord "politics" and "politicians."
Equally significant, one suspects, is the predilection that
Americans seem to have for the hidden-hand argument. In
various forms, at various times, groups of Americans have
taken comfort in the idea that, despite surface appearances,
groups of mysterious and malevolent individuals exist and
"they" are really running things. "They" may be the banks,
the money interests, Wall Street, the trusts, the Socialists,
the Communists, the Jews, or any combination thereof.
Belief in the effectiveness of these hidden elites has not been
restricted to either the liberal or the conservative extremes
of the ideological spectrum. The hidden-hand argument is

as attractive to the lettered as to the unlettered. It seems to satisfy a romantic element in human nature, while providing a simple, dramatic, and psychologically satisfying explanation for the existence of the evils that beset men. At the same time, it qualifies its possessor as a "realist"—one who really knows how things work. "While some of the myths about government are the product of naïveté, others shine with a slick veneer of sophistication. Among the latter is the stereotype picture of myriad lobbyists swarming through the halls of Congress trying to influence legislative decisions."[1]

Stereotyped views of the impact of pressure groups on Congress have been perpetuated and reinforced by journalistic writings and the works of political scientists. The first important scholarly work, and perhaps the best, was Arthur F. Bentley's seminal volume, *The Process of Government,*[2] first published in 1908. This work provided a systematic interpretation of virtually every phase of American political life, including the functioning of Congress, in terms of groups. Despite its many merits, the book had little impact until a later generation. There are several reasons for this, perhaps the most important of which is that the book seemed to be doing little more than systematizing what scholars and laymen already presumed to be the truth: that groups dominated the legislative process. In addition, as a product of the Progressive Era, it had to compete for attention with a variety of dramatic exposés, and its dry style and abstract manner placed it at a serious disadvantage.

Since the Progressive Era, political scientists have often written about interest groups. Fascination with the machinations of the wicked pressure groups may have been mixed with a desire on the part of the authors to demonstrate that they were true "realists." They may have felt that when writ-

1. Bertram M. Gross, *The Legislative Struggle: A Study in Social Combat* (New York: McGraw-Hill Book Co., 1953), p. 223.
2. Bloomington, Indiana: Principia Press, 1949.

ing about so earthy a subject as interest groups they ran no
risk of being considered dwellers in the ivory tower.

The best and most sophisticated recent exposition of the
group interpretation of politics is David Truman's stimulating
volume, *The Governmental Process*.[3] Because the volume
has also been influential, it may be helpful to use it as a
means of illustrating some of the difficulties confronting
those who attempt to deal with Congress solely in terms of
the group approach.

Characteristic of the literature dealing with interest groups
and Congress is a heavy reliance on illustrative examples
and a minimal dependence on quantitative data.[4] The
reason, of course, is perfectly understandable. A writer
who knows that Congress is dominated by interest groups
will naturally seek examples illustrating that truth. If a case
fits his expectations, he will be able to identify it easily as
a useful illustration. As a consequence, the literature on
Congress and interest groups, over a period of time, comes to
consist largely of success stories in which groups get what
they want. The process is self-vindicating. The investigator
postulates the capacity of interest groups to influence Congress, seeks only supporting examples, and is confirmed in his
original postulate when he finds that the data he has gathered
support it.

A case that does not fit the investigator's expectations
will naturally be passed by as not illustrating any point of
significance. Stories of failure are rare in the lore of interest
groups. They are rare, not because failure is rare, but because investigators have not regarded this kind of case as

3. New York: Alfred A. Knopf, Inc., 1958.
4. "Yet in spite of the critical importance of the relationship
between interest groups and law-making institutions, research offers
surprisingly few cumulative or empirical data about this phase of
the representative process." John C. Wahlke, William Buchanan,
Heinz Eulau, and LeRoy C. Ferguson, "American State Legislators'
Role Orientations Toward Pressure Groups," *Journal of Politics*, 22
(1960), 203-27.

significant and have not looked for examples of it. Therefore, while the success stories have been duly recorded and
have been passed on from generation to generation of textbook writers, stories of failure are rarely noted and quickly
interred. Yet failure is no less "fact" because it is failure
than success is "fact" because it is success. If the investigator is to use illustrative examples to demonstrate the
potency of interest groups, he should also seek cases that
will establish the limits of that potency, the circumstances
under which the influence of interest groups is limited. The
difficulty with the interest group interpretation of congressional behavior is not that it lacks factual support but that
so little effort has been devoted to making certain that it
is based upon the *full* range of available fact.

Proponents of the group interpretation of politics have
felt no compulsion to be systematically inclusive in the
use of data. Examples that do not fit their formulations will
be explained away when they are not ignored. In *The
Governmental Process,* the author refers to the case study
prepared by Stephen K. Bailey, *Congress Makes a Law,*[5]
dealing with the events leading to the passage of the Em-
ployment Act of 1946. In this case history, legislators and
their assistants are portrayed in extremely active terms.
They plan the strategy, mobilize group support, induce interest group representatives to testify, and their actions are
decisive for the final passage of a bill. In the *Governmental
Process,* the case is dismissed as atypical "since it involved
few concrete deprivations or indulgences."[6] Nowhere, however, are data introduced that bear on how typical or atypical
the example may actually be. Understanding is rarely ad-
vanced as long as exceptions to a presumed rule are cast aside
as mere sports of nature.

Turning to the substantive difficulties involved in the

5. New York: Columbia University Press, 1950.
6. Truman, p. 342.

group approach, an important problem relates to the mechanics of the relationship between an interest group and Congress. Professor Truman notes that a political interest group cannot achieve power unless it has access to key points in the government. "Access," therefore, becomes his central analytic tool, but he acknowledges that access, by itself, does not give power to the group possessing it: "Moreover, access is not a homogenous commodity. In some forms it provides little more than a chance to be heard; in others it practically assures favorable action."[7]

As it is used in *The Governmental Process*, access is a protean term. Sometimes it is used in a restricted sense to mean no more than communication between two parties; other times, however, it appears to imply not only communication but a successful intrusion into the policy-making process itself. Because the term is freighted with functional ambiguity, it makes unnecessary a serious examination of what happens after a group has achieved access (in the restricted sense) to congressmen. Once "access" in the narrow sense has been demonstrated, "access" in the broader sense is more or less automatically inferred. The dual use of the term helps explain why there has been so little examination of what happens *after* a group achieves access to Congress, although this is obviously the crux of the matter. In practice, despite the demurrers, access is equated with influence.

What are the mechanisms by which access is supposed to be translated into policy? For example, in conference committees, where contention may be sharp and where the final drafting of a bill often takes place, do the views of pressure groups impinge in a significant way, or is the determining factor the action to be expected from the House and from the Senate? An emphasis upon the details of the mechanisms that are presumed to exist is important. One

7. *Ibid.*, p. 321.

source of the confusion that has plagued this area of investigation has been the excessively casual attitude that many writers have taken toward the mechanics of the relationship between interest group and congressman. They refer to the "pressure" an interest group exerts on a congressman, but they rarely go beyond that since the reader is presumed to know what "pressure" is. But does he? He may know what pressure is when the subject under discussion is hydraulics, but what is involved in the concept when it is moved into the realm of human behavior? What is "pressure" when the elements involved consist of a congressman and a spokesman for an interest group? The carefree substitution of an analogy from biology or mechanics for a complex human relationship can generate a great deal of confusion. Men accept the analogy in lieu of a genuine explanation, and they are deterred from probing because the analogue is so simple and satisfying.

Individuals committed to the group approach encounter another difficulty when they approach Congress. The theory more or less requires that Congress and congressmen be treated as passive, for only then is the investigator justified in focusing his attention exclusively on the techniques and dynamics of interest group access to Congress. While the individual using the group approach may be aware of case material that conveys a very different picture of Congress, he can incorporate it into his analysis only at the cost of undermining his central thesis. An activist interpretation of Congress or congressmen and the assumption that "pressure groups" are a major source of political power do not go well together.

The difficulty is nicely exhibited by the reasoning in *The Governmental Process*. Professor Truman disavows an outlook that would treat Congress or individual congressmen as passive. "The politician-legislator is not equivalent to the steel ball in a pinball game, bumping passively from post to post down an inclined plane."[8] He goes on to say, "As indicated by the evidence we have examined, the belief that the relationship between groups and legislators is a one-way, coercive relationship simply does not explain the observed behaviors. The institution of government, as later chapters will further demonstrate, is not so passive and cannot be understood in such oversimplified terms."[9] Nevertheless, Congress virtually disappears except as the arena in which the play of group pressures works itself out. Two chapters in *The Governmental Process* deal with the legislative process, and they are entitled "The Dynamics of Access in the Legislative Process" and "Techniques of Interest Groups in the Legislative Process." Presumably, when one has dealt with the pressures exerted on Congress, there is not much left to say about that body. Congress is not presented as an active, moving, decision-making body but as primarily a recipient of external influences. It is not seen as a body composed of multiple elements jousting for power, influence, jurisdiction, and status on the basis of different policy preferences, but rather as an instrument for registering, weighing, and responding to group pressures.

A curious feature of the writing on Congress by advocates of the group interpretation is that congressmen almost invariably emerge as papier-mâché figures. The reason for this is clear. The requirements of the group interpretation of politics more or less force the writer to strip congressmen of their human qualities. They do not emerge as individuals, many of whom are able, determined, ambitious— with a good deal of freedom of action—but as protoplasmic units having only the characteristics that the theory calls for, *i.e.,* the capacity to register, weigh, and respond to pressure.

When a statement is made about the influence of interest groups in the legislative process, assumptions are neces-

8. *Ibid.,* 332.
9. *Ibid.,* 351.

sarily being made about the behavior of legislators. It cannot be otherwise. What, then, are the implications of the group approach for the behavior of congressmen. If pressure is to be successfully exerted on congressmen by interest groups, the following are requisite:

1. An interest group must take an action designed to induce a congressman to behave in a specific way.
2. The congressman must perceive the action and its source.
3. He must interpret the action correctly as suggesting that he take a specific action or series of actions.
4. He must weigh the suggestion or the "pressure."
5. Finally, he must take the action suggested.

However persuasive and attractive a theory may be in its generalized form, it is unsound if the implied behavior of human actors is not borne out by the facts. Proponents of the group approach appear to have been disinclined to test their theory by juxtaposing its requirements with the actual behavior of congressmen. The vantage point from which they write, for example, is almost invariably that of the interest group. If influence is to exist, however, there must be someone who is influenced as well as someone trying to exert influence. The researcher must ask not only, "Who is talking?" but "Who is listening?" When Shakespeare's Owen Glendower said, "I can call spirits from the vasty deep," Hotspur quickly replied, "Why, so can I, or so can any man; but will they come when you do call for them?" When we see a man in a public market busily hawking his wares, we say that he is "selling" them. We should say, rather, that he is *trying* to sell them. Only if someone is buying, is the seller actually selling. Certainly, the physical activity of the salesman is not a reliable index of sales volume. In much the same way, interest groups are not selling—whatever the level of their activity—unless congressmen are buying. An organization may try to pres-

sure a congressman, but whether he actually feels pressure
is another question. The answer to that question should be
determined, not assumed.

What appears as "pressure" to the outsider may not appear as pressure to the individual thought to be its victim.
One congressman stated: "There are very few people actually pressuring us, even if you count all we hear about all
issues. Seriously the sense of being pressured is a matter of
reaction. Other men who get more mail than we do in this
office would say, 'See how much pressure is on me.' We
don't feel it."[10] The legislator may fail to perceive the actions of an interest group (he is a busy man), may misunder-
stand its communications and fail to realize that he is supposed to feel pressure, may ignore these communications
as insignificant (interest group messages often wind up in
Congressional wastebaskets), or may purposely disregard
them (the group has no effective sanctions at its disposal;
the congressman is hardened to group communications; he
doesn't like the idea that an interest group thinks it can
guide his decisions). To explain the congressman's behavior
in terms of external pressure cannot fail to be misleading
if he does not, himself, feel pressed. It is a mistake to examine the externals of a situation, infer that an individual
must be feeling pressure, and then explain his behavior in
terms of the feelings imputed to him.

To be effective, interest group pressure must work upon
individual congressmen, for they cast the votes that ultimately decide what shall become law and what shall not.
Therefore, one must not only investigate the activities of the
interest groups but the activities of the congressmen. How do
legislators, in fact, react to lobbies, lobbyists, and the actions
associated with them?

A congressman's behavior will be based on his perception

10. Lewis Anthony Dexter, *Congressmen and the People They
Listen To* (Boston: Massachusetts Institute of Technology, 1955), V,
4.

of the total situation in which he finds himself. His perception of interest groups is a part of this total outlook and, as such, will affect his behavior. While his perception of interest groups may influence the entire range of his behavior in marginal ways, it will *govern* his behavior toward interest groups.

Thus far, very little research has been done on the perceptions that congressmen have of interest groups. One explanation for this is that, to the advocates of the group interpretation of Congressional activity, the views of the congressmen are almost irrelevant. If a legislator should assert that he feels no pressure from an interest group, he would be told that this simply illustrates the subtle way in which group pressures work. The congressman is responding to group pressures without even knowing it because he has internalized the values of the group and therefore responds to group influences without realizing it.

> A legislator-politician no less than any other man has . . . lived his life in a series of environments, largely group-defined. These have given him attitudes, frames of reference, points of view, which make him more receptive to some proposals than to others. . . . Many, if not all, such legislators will insist in all sincerity that they vote as their own consciences dictate. They may even resent any effort from an otherwise acceptable group to force a particular decision from them. This is true; however, whether they are "liberals" or "conservatives," urbanites or country boys, their "consciences" are creatures of the particular environments in which they have lived and of the group affiliations they have performed.[11]

This is a useful and attractive line of argument since legislators, like everyone else, do internalize values. Having established a general proposition that is incontrovertible, the

11. Truman, *Governmental Process,* pp. 338-39.

next step is to assume that, of all the values congressmen internalize, it is the group-related values that dominate their behavior. On the basis of this line of analysis the group theorist feels confident in setting aside whatever congressmen may say "in all sincerity" about their own motivations and substituting his own interpretation. The testimony of congressmen, by definition, is beside the point since the bases of their own behavior (*i.e.,* internalized values) are beyond their reach. Only the political analyst knows what "really" leads congressmen to behave as they do.

The question of "pressure" and its relation to internalized values can be clarified if several simple distinctions are made. First, a congressman either has or has not internalized a given set of group-related values. Second, demands relating to that set of values either are or are not made upon him. Combining the two factors, values and demands, allows for the construction of a simple four-cell matrix.

	Values Internalized	Values Not Internalized
No Demands Made	1 Values Internalized No Demands Made	2 Values Not Internalized No Demands Made
Demands Made	3 Values Internalized Demands Made	4 Values Not Internalized Demands Made

"Pressure" does not exist unless (1) demands for action are made of the legislator and (2) the values incorporated in the demand are not internalized by the legislator. Thus, only cell 4, above, constitutes true pressure. Cells 1, 2, and 3 are irrelevant to claims of interest group potency. If interest groups are to live up to the role traditionally ascribed to them, they must have the capacity to alter a legislator's behavior and not merely to reinforce it. It is no test of the strength of the Farm Bureau Federation, for example, when it urges an Iowa congressman to vote for farm support prices. The acid test would come if an interest group tried to persuade a congressman to do its bidding when he had not internalized the interests of the group and when, in fact, he adhered to a conflicting set of values. Since the making of demands is thought to be a characteristic of interest groups, only cells 3 and 4 are relevant to their position. That is, the only question is whether or not the congressman has internalized the set of values lying behind the demands.

While the scholarly literature on Congress and on interest groups has for many years emphasized the importance of the latter at the expense of the former, it should be pointed out that a few writers have broken with this view, either explicitly or inferentially. *Congress at Work*[12] by Stephen Bailey and Howard Samuel is sprinkled with examples that suggest the limited effectiveness, under various circumstances, of party, constituency, and interest group pressure on congressmen. Stephen Bailey's *Congress Makes a Law* is one prolonged account of Congressional activism that is far removed from the role attributed to Congress by the group theorists.

The Legislative Struggle by Bertram Gross was written on the basis of extensive first-hand experience with the workings of Congress. It suggests that initiative and drive in the legislative process derive from the Executive Branch and Congress. Interest groups appear to be on the periphery in most struggles and emerge as the manipulated more often than as the manipulators. Harmon Zeigler's fine study, *Interest Groups in American Society*,[13] is an important addition to the literature. In his excellent study, *Congressmen and the People They Listen To,* Lewis Anthony Dexter examined the problem of pressure from the point of view of the congressman: "This is simply the fact that most of them do not

12. New York: Henry Holt & Co., 1952.
13. Englewood Cliffs, New Jersey: Prentice-Hall, 1964.

see themselves as under pressure when the outsider, nurtured in the notions of Lincoln Steffens, the realistic political parties textbook, and the exposés appearing in *The New Republic* or *The Reporter* of oil or trucking in politics, would think they must be."[14] On the matter that he studied (the reciprocal trade issue in 1953, 1954, and 1955) "the overwhelming majority of the Congressmen were free to vote any way they chose. . . ."[15]

Bernard C. Cohen's pamphlet, *The Influence of Non-Governmental Groups on Foreign Policy Making*,[16] surveyed the literature bearing on the role of interest groups in foreign policy. He notes that the data needed to support the interpretations made concerning the role of interest groups in the foreign policy field have never been gathered.

> A substantive and thus more serious weakness in this body of literature is that very little of it is the product of empirical research, or deals with concrete evidence; instead, most of it rests on or reflects traditional opinion and interpretation—academic as well as public—in assigning weights to various types of organized groups. As a result a "legend" of pressure group potency in foreign policy appears to be accepted and passed on without evidence to new generations of students and researchers.[17]

Others have remarked, in passing, on the relative weakness of interest groups in the foreign policy field. Roger Hilsman[18] notes that there are relatively few interest groups at work on foreign policy, and those that do exist focus mainly on the question of tariff protection. He states categorically, "Congress has a greater freedom in the field of

14. Vol. V, 2.
15. Vol. VI, 22.
16. Boston: World Peace Foundation, 1959.
17. *Ibid.,* p. 2.
18. "Congressional-Executive Relations and the Foreign Policy Consensus," *American Political Science Review,* LII, No. 3 (Sept., 1958), 728.

foreign policy than is ordinarily supposed."[19] Samuel Huntington makes somewhat the same main point in *The Common Defense: Strategic Programs in National Politics.*[20] Both assume, interestingly, that in the policy areas that they have not examined, interest groups are probably strong.

The most important empirical contribution to the field in recent years is Lester Milbrath's splendid volume, *The Washington Lobbyists.*[21] Milbrath's focus is on lobbyists and their activities rather than upon Congressional perceptions of lobbying activity, but he does deal with the impact of lobbying on governmental decisions in Chapter XVII. His findings have much in common with those presented in this study.

> When lobbyists work on broad national policy, their effect is very minor. Lobbyists are effective when they are urging what you are for and not effective when they are urging what you are not for. I have watched people come and go on the Hill here for fourteen years, and I have seldom seen a change in a fellow's basic philosophy even though he has been subject to all sorts of pressures. . . . Lobbying might have some effect on insignificant facets of legislation, but it doesn't have much effect on the philosophy of a senator. The longer a senator has been here, the more he is convinced the people back home like his philosophy and the less susceptible he is to lobbying. . . .
>
> I think over the long haul that lobbying hasn't too much influence. I think they do have some impact on the details, and considerable impact on specialized legislation.[22]

It may seem strange that the interpretation of Congressional behavior in terms of interest group activity should have to be combatted when it was never established in the

19. *Ibid.*, p. 727.
20. New York: Columbia University Press, 1961, p. 147.
21. Chicago: Rand McNally, 1963.
22. *Ibid.*, pp. 337, 344.

first place. Nevertheless, that is the way it is with elements
incorporated into the mythology of a society. When a belief has long been honored, however uncertain its founda-
tions, the burden of proof necessarily rests with its critics.
It would be unfortunate, however, if the attempt to counter
this exaggeration resulted in an overstatement in the opposite
direction. Organized groups have been important in the
past, are important now, and will play a role in the future.
The question is not whether organized groups have influence
in Congress—they do. The real question revolves around
the *conditions* under which groups sometimes have influence
and sometimes do not. Detailed information is needed
about their effectiveness under varying conditions, and a
strenuous effort must be made to separate fact from fancy.

The effort to shrink interest groups to life size should
not be interpreted as a criticism of the role that interest
groups play. Their position is an assured one and is
thoroughly legitimate. Lobbying is not bad in itself; unfortunate decisions may result from lobbying but so may
fortunate ones. Lobbying should certainly not be con-
demned wholesale because an observer disapproves of a
particular piece of legislation influenced by an interest group.

A closer scrutiny of Congressional perceptions of interest
group activity may help to dissolve some of the myths and
stereotypes that surround the relationship between congressman and interest group. A number of important questions
need to be asked. The answers cannot be found by inference
but must be based on investigation. To this end, congressmen were asked questions designed to illuminate the following: Are freshman congressmen and relative newcomers
more or less susceptible than old-timers to the requests of
organized groups? Do congressmen from safe districts
behave differently vis-à-vis interest groups than those from
unsafe districts? How effective is an interest group when a
legislator has not internalized its value system? How effective

is an interest group if it lacks significant strength in the congressman's district? Are there some substantive areas in which interest groups are more effective than in others? In what ways has the relationship of interest groups to Congress changed over the years? Has there been an ebb and flow of influence? Do congressmen with certain personality characteristics react differently to interest groups than congressmen with other characteristics?

This study is not an over-all examination of Congressional voting. It does not set out to explain why congressmen vote as they do but rather attempts to determine the influence of interest groups on Congressional voting. If it should demonstrate that group influence on Congressional voting is less powerful than customarily assumed, the functioning of Congress and the behavior of congressmen will have to be regarded in an altered perspective. Since Congress plays an important role in the American system of government, changes in men's ideas about its functioning must necessarily raise questions about the operation of the entire governmental system, including the means for harmonizing conflicting group interests and the means for achieving policies in the national interest.

Chapter 2

Congressmen Look at Groups

Peripheral Interests

Politicians spend their lives "seeing people," hearing their views on current questions, and presenting their own. That is their daily life. Congressmen, as politicians, spend time talking with people—those with whom they agree and those with whom they do not agree, members of their party and members of the opposition, colleagues, friends, strangers, the influential and the humble, the saints and the sinners.

This practice of seeing people serves a useful function for the congressman. It is an important means—for some congressmen it is the most important means—by which he maintains contact with the currents that are active in his immediate surroundings and in the more distant parts of his environment. Since the congressman is a member of the national legislature, with the responsibility for making scores of decisions on matters of moment, the assorted bits of information and opinion that come to him as a consequence of seeing people comprise, in many cases, the raw material out of which his decisions are fashioned.

To be sure, seeing people is not merely a source of data that may ultimately influence the decisions a congressman may make; it is also a major part of his professional life during many of his waking hours. A congressman may talk with someone in order to gain information on a pending piece of legislation, but he may also speak with an individual simply because he is sociable. Seeing people is a mode of life often established years before he was elected to Congress, and being a legislator does not change this aspect of his life pattern.

Students of Congressional decision-making will necessarily have a persistent interest in the communications aspect of the day-to-day life of congressmen. With whom do they talk? To whom do they listen most carefully? What things do they read? Among the many persons with whom congressmen talk are representatives of organized interest groups. How do congressmen perceive the contacts they have with interest groups, and what influence do these contacts have on the behavior of individual congressmen?

A congressman will spend the bulk of his time on a relatively narrow range of legislative interests; that is to say, he will have one or several areas of specialization. If he is not to be hopelessly superficial he must specialize in certain areas, for he will not have the time, energy, and talent to become equally knowledgeable on all issues that may arise. He must be content to know a good deal less about some matters than others. The assignment of congressmen to committees fosters this specialization. At the same time, every congressman is expected to have some familiarity with, and to take positions upon, an extremely broad range of general issues outside his area of specialization. In this study, therefore, reference will be made to the area of a congressman's "working interests," on the one hand, and the area of his "peripheral interests," on the other.

An investigator of Congressional perceptions of interest group activities will be drawn to the following question: Does the congressman have the same attitudes and perceptions regarding interest groups across the entire range of his activities, or are his perceptions of group activity within his working sphere different from his perceptions outside it?

In an attempt to find answers to this question, this chapter will examine the responses of congressmen to queries dealing with issues outside their working interests. There were two categories from which issues of general interest might be taken: (1) those that had become the focus of public and Congressional controversy and (2) those that had received some public and organized group activity but which had not become major storm centers during the 86th Congress. The first category would include the Forand Bill that involved medical care for the elderly, minimum wages, federal aid to education, water pollution, District of Columbia home rule, and a pay raise for federal employees. The category of the less controversial issues included a proposed youth conservation corps, on-site picketing, and the prohibiting of serving alcoholic beverages on commercial airliners.

Only those issues on which a congressman had not worked were considered for discussion. If he had given special attention to the matter, an alternate issue was discussed. In addition, whenever possible, the issue selected was one enjoying attention from organized groups at the time of the interview. There was also an effort to divide interviewing evenly between the more controversial and the less controversial issues. This broke down somewhat, however, when two of the issues selected as noncontroversial became storm centers before the end of the interviewing period. Despite this difficulty, nineteen of the thirty-four congressmen interviewed discussed controversial issues and fifteen, the less controversial. Issues, not bills, were discussed with most congressmen. In some cases, several bills were pending simultaneously that were either identical (the House of Representatives does not permit multiple sponsorship of bills) or not significantly different. The respondents were often unfamiliar with specific bills but were customarily familiar with the broad issues involved. Since they were asked to discuss the contacts by organized groups in a substantive area in which they, by definition, had taken no special interest, it was to be expected that the congressmen would have difficulty discussing the frequency, character, and style of those contacts. Their answers were sometimes brief or vague or both—but were, nonetheless, illuminating.

Frequency and Character of Group Contacts

One of the first points to establish in assessing Congressional perception of interest group activity is the frequency of interest group contact with congressmen. On these issues of peripheral interest, twenty-two of the thirty-four who were interviewed reported that they had had contact with interest groups. Of the twelve congressmen who reported no contact with organized groups, three had been questioned on major issues and nine on the less controversial. Of the twenty-two who did report contact with interest groups, sixteen had been questioned on the more controversial issues of the session. This indicates that congressmen were more likely to be contacted by interest groups concerned with controversial issues than with those less controversial.

Table 1 shows the distribution by number of the organized groups mentioned by the congressmen. Of the twenty-two

TABLE 1. Number of organized groups with whom congressmen reported contact on the nonspecialization measure

Groups Mentioned by Each Congressman	Responses	% Total Responses	Total All Groups Mentioned	% Total All Groups Mentioned
0	12	33	0	0
1	11	31	11	34
2	7	19	14	44
3	1	3	3	9
4	1	3	4	13
5+	—	—	—	—
"Several"[a]	4	11	not known	not known
Total	36[b]	100	32	100

a. Respondents did not specify the number of groups.
b. Two congressmen mentioned one specific group and "several" general groups.

reporting contact with interest groups, the heaviest concentration, by far, was among those reporting only one or two contacts. Only one respondent reported as many as three contacts, and only one as many as four.[1] The average number of contacts with organized groups was 1.6. Since many of the issues under discussion had been active for some time, these congressmen clearly had not been deluged with organized group contacts on issues that fell outside their area of working interest, even when those issues had received a good deal of public attention. It should be recalled, too, that the issues selected were those which were known to be the focus of some interest group activity. On the many issues of lesser importance before Congress during a session, interest group activity scaled downward toward zero.

In order to identify the groups making an approach and to determine their saliency to the congressmen, the respondents were asked to identify each group. These identifica-

1. These responses create some ambiguity, since four congressmen replied that they had had several contacts and could not specify the number.

tions were then examined to see if the term used indicated the general interest of the organization or its specific name. It was assumed that identification of an organized group by its general interest (*i.e.*, farm organization, labor organization) indicates that such a group is less salient to a congressman than one which he identifies by name (*i.e.*, Farm Bureau Federation, AFL-CIO).

TABLE 2. Number of organized groups with whom congressmen reported contact on the nonspecialization measure and identification of group

Groups Mentioned by Each Congressman	Congressmen	% Congressmen	Total Mentioned	% Total Mentioned
		General Interest of Group		
1	10	48	10	42
2	7	33	14	58
3	—	—	—	—
4+	—	—	—	—
"Several"[a]	4	19	not known	not known
Total	21[b]	100	24	100
		Specific Name of Group		
1	4	67	4	50
2	2	33	4	50
3	—	—	—	—
4+	—	—	—	—
"Several"	—	—	—	—
Total	6[b]	100	8	100

a. Respondents did not specify the number of groups.

b. Five congressmen identified organized groups both by the general interest of the group and by the specific name of the group.

Table 2 shows the distribution of these identifications. Only six of the congressmen who had had contacts with organized groups were able to identify the contacting group by name. The remainder of those interviewed identified each group by its general area of interest rather than by specific name. All but five of the organized groups mentioned by name were major, well-known organizations. This suggests that the well-known interest groups are more visible to the congressmen than are the lesser known ones. On the whole, then, it appears that congressmen, in their areas of peripheral interest, have contact with relatively few interest groups, that those which they identify easily are nationally prominent organizations, and that the saliency or visibility of other interest groups tends to be low.

TABLE 3.   Relative group-congressmen policy position on congressmen's nonspecialization measure[a]

Policy Position	General Interest of Group	
	Responses	All Groups Mentioned
Agree	9	9
Agree modification	—	—
Modification	—	—
Disagree	6	6
No clear position	6	9
Total	21	24
	Specific Name of Group	
Agree	2	2
Agree modification	—	—
Modification	—	—
Disagree	2	3
No clear position	2	3
Total	6	8

a. Tabulation excludes responses indicating no contact and responses indicating "Several" groups contacted. Total number of congressmen, 20.

Table 3 seeks to discover if there is a relation between a congressman's identification of a group by name or area of interest and whether he perceives it as agreeing or disagreeing with his own position. It is interesting that the congressmen, in areas in which they had no special competence, did not have a refined or clear-cut view of interest groups and what they stand for. The congressman's inclination to make fine distinctions in the degree of his agreement or disagreement with a group is obviously related to his knowledge of the subject matter and the position of the group. On issues with which he has little familiarity, he will often have no recourse but to rely on general impressions and to say that the group either agrees or disagrees with him, with little shading between these extremes.

The congressmen's tendency to perceive groups as either agreeing with them or not may have resulted from discussing issues rather than specific bills. Likewise, the fact that they did not specify their own policy positions may have been the result of having discussed only issues. It is highly likely that congressmen and interest groups could agree on a general principle on a particular issue but disagree on its specific provisions. For instance, the issue of federal aid to education has, over the years, accumulated several complex and highly controversial specific proposals. It is quite possible that two or more congressmen could agree on the principle that there should be some further action in this field—to use Congressional parlance, that "something should be done" —by the federal government. However, they might disagree vehemently about the level of education receiving such aid, the programs to be included, whether public or public and nonpublic schools should be involved, whether to include racially segregated school systems, and the methods of financing any aid. In addition, each organized group interested in this issue may have a slightly different position on each of these substantive areas included in the issue of federal aid to education.

Moreover, some congressmen are reluctant to give their own policy position on a general issue until they have some knowledge of the provisions of the committee bill relating to that issue. A standing committee can, of course, amend, combine, substitute, or kill any of the bills; only after bills have been reported out of committee can congressmen who are not on the committee vote on them. In fact, one hears tales of the sponsors of legislation who vote against their own bills after the standing committee has "worked its will." Thus, a congressman may favor a principle involved in an issue, but he may also have a number of reasons for opposing a bill reported out of committee. Many congressmen were reluctant to express their own position until they knew the provisions of the specific bill on which they were to vote. For instance, the Forand Bill covered certain kinds of medical care for elderly persons financed through social security, but none of the congressmen outside the Ways and Means Committee could vote on it. The only similar measure reported out of committee and debated on the floor of the House was the Kerr-Mills Bill, and while the latter did cover the general issue of medical care for elderly persons, many of its provisions for medical care differed from the Forand Bill, and the method of financing was substantially different.

TABLE 4. Character of congressmen's contacts with all organized groups mentioned on the nonspecialization measure

Type of Contacts	Times Mentioned	% Mentioned
Mail	20	45
Office call	15	33
Committee	—	—
Telephone	6	14
Discussion session	1	2
Personal talk	—	—
Social engagement	2	4
Telegram	1	2
Read advertisement	—	—
Total	45	100

Table 4 shows the distribution of congressman and interest group contacts by type: mail, office call, committee hearings, telephone, discussion session, personal talk, social engagement, telegram, reading of an advertisement. This breakdown indicates that these contacts were, on the whole, formal and impersonal. Of the contacts, 45 per cent came through the mail. If the mail contacts are combined with telegrams, this means that 47 per cent of the contacts that organized groups have with congressmen do not involve any verbal exchange. Telephone conversations, which involve a verbal exchange but no face-to-face contact, account for another 14 per cent. Taking these categories together, it appears that in the case of 61 per cent of the contacts, there is no face-to-face confrontation between the congressman and the group representative. The office call, which accounts for 33 per cent of interest group contacts, involves face-to-face contact but often under formalized and impersonal circumstances. Typically it would consist of a visit by several of the congressman's constituents accompanied by the legislative representative of a national organization. It is apparent, therefore, that extended personal exchanges between congressmen and interest group representatives are far less frequent than might have been expected in matters that are not the congressmen's first order of business. Consequently, there is lessened opportunity for the interest groups to influence congressmen by means of personal persuasion.

TABLE 5. Estimated frequency and amount of contact with all groups mentioned on the nonspecialization measure

Estimated Frequency and Amount of Contact	Congressmen	% Congressmen
Little	9	41
Some	10	45
Periodic	3	14
Frequent	—	—
Total	22	100

Table 1 dealt with the number of groups that had contacted the congressmen. Table 5 deals with the frequency of these contacts, dividing them into the rough categories of "little," "some," "periodic," and "frequent."[2] Table 5 indicates that nineteen of the twenty-two congressmen (86 per cent) having contact with interest groups on a measure not in their area of working interest had "some" or "little" contact. None of the congressmen had contact that could be described as "frequent," and only three responses fell into the "periodic" category.

TABLE 6. Initiation of organized group-congressmen contacts on the nonspecialization measure

Contact Made by:	Congressmen	% Congressmen
Group	21	95
Congressman	1	5
Mutual/could not distinguish	—	—
Total	22	100

There is another question of equal importance: who initiates contact between organized groups and the congressmen on matters of peripheral interest to the congressmen? Only one of the twenty-two congressmen who reported contact with organized groups indicated that he had initiated the contact (Table 6). This congressman had seen in the newspaper the name of a group that was co-ordinating the effort to gather signatures for the discharge petition on

2. The category of "little" included the statements of congressmen that there had been little contact, that personal contact had been approximately once a year, or that there was scattered mail each week. If a congressman indicated that there was light daily mail, that personal contact was more frequent than once a year but less than once a month, or if he said that there was "some contact," the response would be placed in the category of "some" contact. The classification of "periodic" was used to include those instances in which a congressman had received an organized "flood" of mail on a subject, had received more frequent contacts as a bill became active, or had continuing contact with the group. The category of "frequent" was used when a congressman indicated that he had co-operated actively with a group over a span of some years.

the District of Columbia Home Rule measure. He had telephoned the organization to get information on the measure
itself and to ascertain the group's progress with it. He could
not recall the name of the group, however, and he did not
consider the contact as important in influencing his opinion,
since he had favored the measure before talking to a representative of the interest group. In all other cases, organized
groups made the first contact. The pattern is clear: the group
makes the initial contact on matters that are of peripheral
concern to a congressman, and he normally sees little
reason why he should get in touch with them.

TABLE 7. Congressmen's personal reactions to contacts with organized groups on the nonspecialization measure

Personal Reaction of Congressmen	All Groups Contacted	% All Groups Contacted	Some Groups Contacted
Found Contact			
Informed	11	34	—
Uninformed	1	3	—
Co-operative	1	3	—
Unco-operative	—	—	—
Irritating	1	3	—
Not irritating	7	21	—
Just listened	3	9	—
No reaction	4	12	—
Saw chance to promote own side	5	15	—
Total	33	100	—

Congressmen's Reaction to Organized Groups

So far the discussion has focused only on the number and
characteristics of contacts between congressmen and organized groups, and has not dealt with congressmen's
attitudes toward these groups. Each of those interviewed
was asked to indicate his response to the actions of these
groups and his estimate of their importance. The respondents
showed an initial neutral reaction to these groups on the
whole, neither approving nor disapproving. Interest group

contact was simply accepted as an expected part of Congressional routine.

In order to elicit a wider range of personal reactions, the congressmen were also asked to indicate whether they felt that the groups were uninformed, co-operative, irritating, and so on. Table 7 registers their responses. Once again, the responses indicated approval, on the whole, of the activities of the groups, but their approval seemed contingent on whether the organization provided useful information. Of the 34 per cent who indicated belief that the groups or their representatives were "informed," the responses ranged from slight agreement to emphatic agreement. However, all eight congressmen who *volunteered* favorable comments on these interest groups mentioned that they valued the information supplied by the groups on an issue or on public opinion relating to an issue. Congressmen, in this sample, either regarded interest groups as an asset to them or, at the very least, as an acceptable fact of Congressional life. Adverse reactions tended to be specific and to be related to the activities or approaches of specific groups or to specific incidents.

For example, one congressman said that sometimes interest group representatives come into his office and conduct themselves in an overbearing way. His response is to insult them right back, he said. No one should come into his office and expect him to be a "yes" man. He told several of these representatives that they were doing themselves more harm than good because their actions tempted him to vote against the bill they were supporting, even though he actually favored it.

Importance of Groups

The congressmen interviewed were also asked in an open-ended question to estimate the over-all importance of the interest groups to the legislative progress of the measure

TABLE 8. Congressmen's estimate of the importance of all organized groups with whom they had contact on the nonspecialization measure

Estimated Importance of Groups Contacted	Congressmen	% Congressmen
Very important	6	27
Moderately important	6	27
Not very important	1	5
Unimportant	1	5
Couldn't judge	7	31
Don't know	1	5
Total	22	100

under discussion. Table 8 shows that most of the congressmen who reported contact with organized groups on this measure attributed at least some importance to the activities of these groups, but it also shows that a substantial proportion of the congressmen either could not evaluate or did not know the importance of these groups. Of the replies, 52 per cent indicated that the groups were either moderately important or very important, and 36 per cent indicated that they did not know how important the groups were or could not judge.

A critical question, for the purposes of this study, is whether the congressmen felt pressure from interest groups on issues outside their working sphere. It was clear from the nature of the responses that the respondents did not feel pressure from groups on these measures. Nineteen of the twenty-two congressmen who had had contact with organized groups on the measure under discussion said that they had felt no pressure from these groups. One respondent indicated that he had felt pressure from one group but not from any of the others; another congressman had had such slight contact with the interest groups that the question of pressure was not asked. Yet another remarked that, when he had left his home town to come to Congress, he expected to be subjected to a lot of pressure. Now that he was here, he said, he kept waiting for the pressure to begin. There wasn't much of it, and any man who couldn't withstand that small an amount had no business being in Congress. Of the 19 congressmen, only one fitted the stereotype of the legislator harried by lobbyists; he indicated that he had felt pressure from all of the groups that had contacted him.

The findings on this question are interesting in the light of the responses to the preceding question. On the one hand, a relatively large number of congressmen agreed that interest groups were important on the peripheral measure that they discussed; on the other hand, the same congressmen were almost unanimous in stating that they had not felt pressure from these groups. Do the answers conflict? How could a congressman regard a group as important or influential and then go on to say that he had felt no pressure from it?

An analysis of the detailed responses of the congressmen, indicating that a group was "very important" to the progress of a particular measure, casts some light on the grounds on which they based their judgment:

1. The national prominence of the organization was important. A well-known group was far more likely to have effectiveness imputed to it than a less well-known group.

2. If the position and activity of a group on an issue were well-known, the respondents more or less automatically placed a high estimate on that group's effectiveness.

3. A group was more likely to be rated important if it was involved in a controversial issue than a noncontroversial issue.

4. When congressmen knew that a group had been carrying on an ambitious public relations campaign, their estimate of that group's effectiveness on the issue at hand tended to go up.

5. If the congressmen agreed with the interest group's

policy position, his estimate of its importance was likely to be high.

In short, an estimate of the importance of an interest group to a dispute inside Congress was likely to be heavily influenced by the congressmen's impressions of that group's activities *outside* Congress. The congressmen seemed to be making the tacit assumption that the prominence or activity of a group in society at large would somehow be translated into influence within the halls and committee rooms of the Capitol. In gauging the importance of a group in a legislative battle, they appeared automatically to make allowance for the group's indirect influence.

The evidence indicates that most congressmen do not feel they are significantly influenced by mail they have reason to believe was stimulated by interest groups. Yet, on this question, they frequently cited a heavy flow of mail as evidence that a group is important. Several explanations for the incongruity present themselves. A congressman who cites the flow of interest group mail as evidence of a group's importance may calculate that, while he is not influenced by this kind of overture, others are likely to be. Another explanation, more in keeping with the tenor of the other observations made in connection with this question, is that when congressmen see activity on the part of organized groups, they assume that this activity, in some way, adds up to influence.

In examining the list of factors that led congressmen to term a group "very important" or "moderately important," it appears that they were making this judgment, to a large extent, on the basis of the saliency of the group involved, the distinctiveness of its stand, and the amount of organization activity perceived by them. The congressmen were really passing judgment on the prominence of the public relations activity of the group and not its success in exerting "pressure." In this way, a group could be deemed "im-

portant" while still having little capacity to exert pressure
on individual congressmen. The group, of course, would
normally take credit for a congressman's vote whether or
not he was influenced by its actions. One congressman put
it this way: "Three teachers telephoned me about the
Thompson Bill [federal aid for school construction]. They
were for it. I also got some mail from teachers' organizations. I don't know how I'm going to vote on the bill
yet. Maybe I'll support it and maybe not. If it goes
through, however, the teachers' organizations will write to
their members taking credit for its passage. But maybe a
lot of Congressmen voted for it because they thought it was
a good bill, and the mail was unimportant."

Thirteen of the congressmen who said they had not
felt pressure attempted to indicate why they had not. In
most cases, they simply viewed the interest group as a source
of information and opinion, and it scarcely occurred to
them to view it as a source of pressure. Others, however,
gave answers indicating that, while they had not felt pressure, they might have under other circumstances; for example, if the bill under discussion had been at a different
stage in its development or if the group had not already
known that the congressman was on its side.

Summary

What, in sum, is the picture that emerges from these
data concerning congressmen's perceptions of interest group
activities on matters peripheral to their sphere of interest?
It is clear that only a few groups do contact a congressman on
a given issue, even when that issue is controversial and the
controversy extends over a substantial period of time, and
that these groups make such contacts rather infrequently.
The image of the congressman as an individual besieged by
lobbyists is patently not borne out by the evidence presented thus far. The range in the types of contacts between

congressman and interest group is quite narrow. There is little face-to-face contact between congressman and interest group and even less opportunity for extended personal exchange.

The neutrality that characterizes the attitude of many congressmen toward interest groups and their lack of interest in these groups are apparently to be explained either by the fact that groups do not appear relevant to the congressmen's interests or are unfamiliar to them.

Chapter 3

Congressmen Look at Groups

Working Interests

During its early history, the House of Representatives was of a homey, comfortable size; its members knew one another and often had the opportunity to pass the time of day. Men, freight, and messages moved slowly at that time, but this created no particular problem, for so did the pace of events in the small and sparsely populated nation that was the United States. The conduct of such foreign relations as the nation had belonged to the President, and the responsibility for the management of the economic life of the nation was not yet conceived to be a governmental responsibility, even though the government did in fact take certain actions that affected the nation's economic development. The issues brought before the legislature were few, and fewer still were the important ones. When an issue of moment, such as slavery, tariffs, or territorial acquisitions, came before this House, other business was set aside so that the members might have ample time to acquaint themselves with the problem and the arguments concerning the proposed remedies. The issue would be debated at length on the floor of the House, and scarcely a legislator could be found who had not followed the deliberations with considerable attention or who had not himself participated in the discussions.

No member of the House of Representatives today has the energy, knowledge, time, or the breadth of interest to be familiar with the full range of complex issues that the twentieth century has thrust upon the Congress. A congressman has no alternative at present but to direct his attention to some areas of action and not to others. By narrowing the scope of his attention, however, he gains increased knowledge of a more restricted area at the expense of a strong grasp of the complexities of broader areas.

Before each congressman was interviewed, an effort was made to determine a major area of specialization as a preliminary to examining in depth his views on one particular measure. The choice of the specific bill discussed was made by the interviewer in order to save time during the interview itself and in order to eliminate the possibility of the congressman's selecting a bill that he regarded as a good example of interest group pressure. This approach had the dual advantage of probing in depth a congressman's views on a matter with which he was familiar, while at the same time covering a wide range of possible group-Congressional relationships over a variety of issues. It is, of course, possible that the selection of specific bills in the area of working interest and the use of issues in the area of peripheral interest affected the comparability of the responses, but it can have had only a relatively minor impact.

Frequency and Character of Group Contacts

Most of the congressmen showed no hesitation during the interviews in discussing their contacts with organized groups. Thirty of the thirty-four congressmen interviewed stated that they had had some contact with interest groups in connection with their specialization measure (Table 9),

TABLE 9. Number of organized groups with whom congressmen reported contact on the specialization measure

Groups Mentioned by Each Congressman	Congressmen	% Congressmen	Total Groups Mentioned	% Total Groups Mentioned
0	4	12	0	0
1	4	12	4	4
2	2	6	4	4
3	6	17	18	20
4	9	26	36	39
5+	4	12	30[a]	33
"Several"[b]	5	15	not known	not known
Total	34	100	92	100

a. One respondent mentioned six groups, two respondents mentioned seven groups, one respondent mentioned ten groups.
b. Respondents did not specify the number of groups.

and twenty-five of these were able to specify the number of groups involved—a total of ninety-two organized groups, or an average of 3.68 groups per congressman. This figure is strikingly low when it is considered that the congressman's area of working interest—whatever it might be—would be of special concern to a number of interest groups. A congressman who specialized in a particular area, and who was probably on the appropriate committees, would be strategically located to advance or impede the interests of various organized groups, and because of his strategic position, one would expect that he would be a high-priority target.

Many congressmen had difficulty identifying interest groups by name. When they were asked to name the groups that had contacted them, twenty-four of the thirty who had had contact with organized groups identified the group by general interest. Only sixteen identified one or more of the groups by name (Table 10). Obviously, several congressmen identified groups both by general interest and by organization name. When they identified a group by name, it was likely to be one with which they had worked closely or to be a major labor, farm, or business organization.

TABLE 10. Number of organized groups with whom congressmen reported contact on the specialization measure and identification of group

Groups Mentioned by Each Congressman	Congressmen	% Congressmen	Total Mentioned	% Total Mentioned
General Interest of Group				
1	4	17	4	8
2	7	29	14	26
3	6	25	18	33
4+	3	12	18[a]	33
"Several"[b]	4	17	not known	not known
Total	24[c]	100	54	100
Specific Name of Group				
1	5	31	5	13
2	3	19	6	16
3	4	25	12	32
4+	3	19	15[d]	39
"Several"	1	6	not known	not known
Total	16[c]	100	38	100

a. Two respondents mentioned four groups each; one respondent mentioned ten groups.

b. Respondents did not specify the number of groups.

c. Ten congressmen identified organized groups both by the general interest of the group and by the specific name of the group.

d. Two respondents mentioned four groups each; one respondent mentioned seven groups.

Many congressmen, having difficulty remembering the names of the interest groups involved, helpfully volunteered to turn to their files as a means of refreshing their memories. Such offers were not accepted since the subject under investigation was the congressman's perception of these groups, their activities, and their impact upon him as a member of the House of Representatives. If group actions on a measure for which a congressman had worked impinged so lightly on his memory that he could not even recall its name without recourse to his files, then its impact upon him must have been slight indeed. In an area with which he is familiar, it seems safe to assume that only those groups within easy range of his memory are likely to have had a real impact upon him.

This inability to identify groups by name suggests that many congressmen are not really attuned to individual groups but tend to think of them in terms of the broader interests that a group claims to represent. Thus, the congressman may speak of "the farmers" or "the business interests," but the formal interest organizations associated with these broad areas tend to be relatively undifferentiated in his mind. Only a handful of organizations—usually large and well-known—appear to be sufficiently salient to be treated as distinct and separate organizations. The others are stripped of their individual identity, so to speak, by the congressman and placed in a category with organizations having common interests. In addition, the congressmen viewed the broad substantive areas in surprisingly unrefined terms. The categories they used were usually those provided by the traditional tripartite division into farm, labor, and business groups.

The fact that many congressmen find it difficult—and in some cases impossible—to remember the names of interest groups with which they have dealt does violence to the stereotype of a congressman who is pulled this way and that by pressure groups.

An effort was made to see whether the ability of a congressman to identify a group by name was related in any way to the policy position of that group, so each was asked to identify those groups that agreed with his policy position and those that did not. Table 11 indicates that the congress-

TABLE 11. Relative group-congressmen policy position on congressmen's specialization measure[a]

Policy Position	Responses	% Responses	All Groups Mentioned	% All Groups Mentioned
General Interest of Group				
Agree	9	39	20	37
Agree modification	4	17	7	13
Modification	2	9	13	24
Disagree	3	13	5	9
No clear position	5	22	9	17
Total	23	100	54	100
Specific Name of Group				
Agree	11	58	26	68
Agree modification	1	5	1	3
Modification	1	5	1	3
Disagree	5	27	8	21
No clear position	1	5	2	5
Total	19	100	38	100

a. Tabulation excludes responses indicating no contact and responses indicating "Several" groups contacted. Total number of congressmen, 25.

men were more often able to identify by name groups that agreed with them than those that differed. This may be explained on psychological grounds in part, but a second factor intrudes. A congressman sometimes works actively with a group on measures that they both support, while he does not have this close contact with groups that oppose him. In other words, he may be more aware of the group not only because it agrees with him but because the agreement that exists generates a closer association than would otherwise exist. It appears that congressmen find it easy to identify by name those groups that agree with them and with which they have worked closely, less easy to name those that agree with them but with which they have not worked closely, and less easy still to name those groups with which they do not agree.

TABLE 12. **Character of congressmen's contacts with all organized groups mentioned on the specialization measure**

Type of Contacts	Times Mentioned	% Times Mentioned
Mail	23	25
Office call	21	23
Committee	17	18
Telephone	13	14
Discussion session	6	7
Personal talk	4	4
Social engagement	5	5
Telegram	3	3
Read advertisement	1	1
Total	93	100

However, five of the twenty-five congressmen identified groups by organization name when they perceived those groups as disagreeing with them. A sustained controversy over a measure in which a congressman is interested will focus his attention on opposing groups and heighten their visibility to him. In addition, if the group has a significant membership within his constituency, he is likely to be thoroughly aware of it. If a congressman agrees with a group and if that group has a following in his constituency, he is likely to develop informal relations with its leadership. His relation with groups that are in opposition to him, however, will tend to be formal and restricted.

What is the character of the contacts between interest groups and a congressman in his area of working interest, and how often do these contacts occur? Table 12 shows the distribution of contacts by type. While the mail remains the single most common form of contact, the opportunity for personal discussion and face-to-face contact appears to be substantially greater in the area of a congressman's working interest than in areas not of special interest to him. Next in order of frequency are office calls, contact through committee testimony, and telephone conversations.

In their areas of working interest, the congressmen were expected to have rather frequent and close contact with a number of groups, but the data reveal the surprising infrequency of such contacts (Table 13). Of the thirty inter-

TABLE 13. Estimated frequency and amount of contact with all groups mentioned on the specialization measure

Estimated Frequency and Amount of Contact	Congressmen	% Congressmen
Little	14	47
Some	6	20
Periodic	6	20
Frequent	4	13
Total	30	100

viewed who had had contacts with organized groups, fourteen, or almost one-half, said they had had "little" contact with these groups—*i.e.*, the groups had written them a few letters or there had been some contact through committee testimony or some annual event. When the categories of "little" contact and "some" contact are combined, over two-thirds of the responses are accounted for. In addition, it should be remembered that some of the contacts included in the tabulation are more ritualistic than substantive. For example, a number of committees take up the same kinds of bills each year, and the same organizations appear before them each year to offer the same arguments. An organization may also mount a mail campaign when a bill has reached a certain stage in its legislative progress. There is little expectation on anyone's part, under these circumstances, that the thinking of the congressmen will be significantly affected.

Only 13 per cent of the congressmen considered their contacts with organized groups to be "frequent." Some of the contacts classified as frequent represented contacts of a close, co-operative nature that might extend over a period of years. A congressman-group relationship of such stability is more rare than might be expected; more typically, a congressman will have scattered contacts with interest groups, and these will remain vague in his memory.

The question of who initiates contacts between congressmen and organized groups is an interesting one. Twenty of the thirty questioned indicated that the group had initiated the contact. Only one congressman said that he had initiated the contact, and he had done so in the hope that the group might provide him with information. In eight cases, however, the congressmen indicated that it was impossible for them to say who had initiated the contact. When a relationship has been stable over a period of time, the parties to it may well find it impossible to recall who initiated it. In such cases, when both parties have had ample opportunity to break off the relationship and have not done so, the relationship is obviously of continuing mutual benefit, and the question of who initiated it in the first instance is, therefore, of little consequence.

In some cases, contact by a group had occurred after a congressman had introduced a bill important to its interests. Although the group initiated the contact with the congressman, it was, in fact, responding to his previous action. Despite the fact that members of the group stood to benefit from passage of the bill, the initiative was taken by the congressman and the interest group played, at best, a supportive role. While the number of these cases is too small to allow any firm conclusion, the examples do suggest that it is a fairly common pattern for interest group support to coalesce around a bill after it has been introduced rather than to work actively for its introduction. It is also interesting as well as suggestive of the congressman's attitude toward interest groups, that in none of these cases did the congressman feel that the support a group could give him was sufficient to impel him to consult with the group in the drafting stage or inform the group that he was going to introduce a bill relating to its interests.

On the whole, as Table 14 reveals, congressmen let

TABLE 14. Initiation of organized group-congressmen contacts on the specialization measure

Contact Made by	Congressmen	% Congressmen
Group	20	67
Congressman	1	3
Mutual/could not distinguish	8	27
Don't know	1	3
Total	30	100

interest groups come to them. A congressman will emphasize that he is happy to talk with anyone who comes to see him, and he takes it for granted that if a group is really concerned with a measure on which he is working, it will seek him out.

In Chapter II, it was observed that congressmen appear to accept interest groups as a fact of their professional life, neither approving of them strenuously nor disapproving. The responses concerning their own interest areas, however, do reveal two sensitive points. First, while most congressmen accepted the possibility of initiating a contact with an interest group, several of them rejected the idea vigorously, indicating that it would be, in some way, improper. Secondly, while only a few congressmen had close, co-operative, and continuing relations with an interest group, there was no hint from most of them that such a relationship might be viewed as irregular. Thus, while a few seemed to feel that a close working relationship between a congressman and an interest group would not be altogether appropriate, most congressmen accepted the legitimacy of active Congressional-group co-operation.

TABLE 15. Congressmen's personal reactions to contacts with organized groups on the specialization measure

Personal Reaction of Congressmen	All Groups Contacted	% All Groups Contacted	Some Groups Contacted	% Some Groups Contacted
Found Contact				
Informed	16	38	4	30
Uninformed	2	5	3	23
Co-operative	10	24	3	23
Unco-operative	—	—	1	8
Irritating	1	2	1	8
Not irritating	7	17	—	—
Just listened	3	7	—	—
No reaction	3	7	1	8
Total	42	100	13	100

Congressmen's Reaction to Organized Groups

When asked about their personal reactions toward organized groups in their area of working interest, the responses of the congressmen were generally neutral in tone, as they were when asked about groups outside their special area of interest. In an effort to elicit more detailed responses, the interviewer asked whether the congressmen found the groups helpful and co-operative or irritating and unco-operative. Once again, there were few negative comments about interest groups in general, although there were some negative comments about particular groups (Table 15). Congressional reaction is, on the whole, positive and favorable, with considerable stress being placed on the information function performed by these groups. For instance, one congressman said that while lobbyists have a bad reputation, their role is justified since they perform valuable research on legislative problems. Another congressman said that the groups tried to keep him well-informed and that, therefore, he gave them his support. By and large, the congressmen's comments did not stress the role that groups played in the broad process of representative government; instead, the groups were seen as a useful adjunct to the legislative process because of their information-providing functions.

The positive comments included volunteered statements that the groups were "co-operative," "effective," "fair," "sincere," "anxious to help," and that they "do best when they limit themselves to facts and figures." However, the congressmen assume that the "facts and figures" supplied by an interest group are reliable only in the sphere of the group's major interest. The congressmen appear to react favorably to organized groups when the latter are quiet, provide useful information, try to be helpful, and show the proper respect for Congressional status.

The negative comments of the congressmen concerning interest groups were never critical of their existence or the role they played but only of specific groups or certain of their practices. For example, one congressman complained in eloquent terms about certain groups that flood his office with stimulated mail, send persons from the district to sit in the gallery of the House of Representatives to scrutinize his voting, or send friends to his office in an effort to elicit a commitment from him on a given issue. Another congressman expressed an adverse reaction to a group that merely wanted to enlarge its own government program; a third congressman reacted unfavorably toward a group that, he claimed, did not represent its own membership in the district or the real opinions of the organization.

Occasionally, a congressman stated that an organized group did not know what it was talking about. One congressman spoke of the so-called Harris Bill that would have changed provisions relating to the retirement of railroad workers: "I received a lot of letters telling me to vote for the Harris Bill because it would help the railroad workers. Well, I knew that most of these letters came from some organization. But by the time that bill came out of committee, it had been so thoroughly changed that it no longer favored the railway workers. But do you know, I continued to get letter after letter telling me to vote for that bill because it would help the railroad workers."

Another congressman discussed the trials and tribulations he endured when his committee was working on the District of Columbia Home Rule Bill: "This young woman chased me from one end of the building to the other. She buttonholed me in the hallways and in my office, and I thought she was going to follow me into the men's room. She was working for a group that was lobbying for D.C. Home Rule. Finally I told her, 'Young lady, you don't know what you're talking about and don't know the difference between the amendment and the Home Rule Bill itself. You have made up my mind for me, however, and I'm going to do the opposite of what you want.' "

The practices most commonly criticized were those that the congressman thought showed lack of respect for his intelligence and position. It appears not to be a specific act, as such, that provokes a congressman so much as what he takes to be the underlying attitude toward Congress and the congressman that the act seems to suggest. A case in point would be the congressman who reacted with displeasure toward a group of representatives who, he said, apparently expected him to be a "yes" man and who treated members of his staff with discourtesy. If, by anything it says or does, an organized group indicates that it believes a congressman can be threatened or coerced, it is likely to precipitate his disapproval. He appears to be saying, in effect, "I am glad to hear what you and your membership think on this issue, and I am glad to have any other information you may be able to provide me with. Do not, however, make the mistake of going beyond the reporting and information functions by trying to tell me how to vote. Above all, if you value my good opinion, do not try to tell me what you will do to me if I don't vote your way."

The responses of those who were interviewed, when asked whether or not they had experienced pressure from interest groups, suggest that congressmen usually feel little pressure from this source. Twenty-eight of the thirty congressmen who had had some contact with organized groups in their area of working interest said that they had not felt pressured or coerced by any of the contact groups. In other words, 93 per cent of the congressmen having contact with these groups felt no pressure from them! Two congressmen reported that they had felt pressured by one group with which they had had contact but had not from any of the other groups. In one case, the group disagreed with the stand of the congressman; in the other case, the group was hoping for some modification of a bill over which the congressman's committee had jurisdiction. An additional congressman said he had not *felt* pressure from the organized groups involved, but he thought they had tried to pressure him.

In trying to explain why they felt no pressure, some of those questioned explained that the relationship between them and an interest group was co-operative or functional and that pressure played no part in it. Interest groups were pleased to present information and opinion, and congressmen were pleased to receive both. Other congressmen explained the lack of pressure in terms of special circumstances such as the following:

1. The relationship between the congressman and the group (*i.e.*, he had an alliance with the group since they were also trying to push the legislation; the group had no leverage in the congressman's district; he disagreed with the position of the group and hence could not be moved by it);

2. The congressman's own position (*i.e.*, long tenure in the House; the congressman strongly favored the bill);

3. The bill itself (the bill did not contain anything that the group would object to).

The implication in these replies was that, given these circumstances, any attempt to exert pressure would have been useless or even injurious to the group. There is also, of course, the tacit suggestion that under other circumstances pressure might have been brought to bear.

TABLE 16. Congressmen's estimate of the importance of all organized groups with whom they had contact on the specialization measure

Estimated Importance of Groups Contacted	Congressmen	% Congressmen
Very important	8	27
Moderately important	7	23
Not very important	10	33
Unimportant	3	10
Couldn't judge	2	7
Total	30	100

Importance of Groups

The congressmen were asked to estimate the impact of interest groups on the outcome of legislation in their area of working interest. Most of the respondents could and did make such estimates (Table 16). Twenty-five of the thirty congressmen who had had some contact with interest groups indicated that individual groups had, or would have, some effect on the course of this legislation. Of the respondents, 50 per cent attributed either "moderate" or "high" importance to the groups' role, while 43 per cent said that their role was "unimportant" or "not very important."

In the cases in which the congressmen felt that a group was very important, one or more of the following conditions were likely to exist:

1. The activities of the group outside Congress were clearly visible to the congressman;

2. Congressman and interest group had a close working relationship;

3. Both congressman and interest group had a strong commitment to legislative results, whether they agreed with each other or not;

4. The group had been a highly reliable source of information;

5. The interest group had a record of long and active support for a measure under consideration.

Those congressmen who made the judgment that interest groups were "moderately" important appeared to combine a relatively low estimate of the effectiveness of the particular groups under discussion with a high estimate of the general effectiveness of group activity. The congressmen who said that the groups were "not very important" or "unimportant" to the outcome of the process appeared to base this judgment on the low visibility of interest groups plus ancillary considerations. These included items such as the following:

1. The congressman, not an interest group, had initiated the bill;

2. The attention of the interest group had been stimulated and activated by the congressman;

3. The congressman had had little contact with the group during the course of the legislative trial;

4. The interest group was divided on the bill;

5. The concerns of the group were tangential to the central issues involved in the bill;

6. The interest group was politically insignificant because it was too narrowly based geographically or because of some other factor;

7. The support for the bill, or the sentiment against it, was so strong in Congress that the preferences of the group would be irrelevant to the outcome.

It is interesting that none of the congressmen who felt that interest groups were unimportant or not very important in their area of working interest related this feeling to any general estimation of the importance of interest groups in the legislative process.

TABLE 17. Congressmen's estimate of committee attention to all of the organized groups on the specialization measure

Estimated Committee Attention to Groups	Congressmen on Committee		Congressmen Not on Committee	
	Con-gressmen	% Con-gressmen	Con-gressmen	% Con-gressmen
Committee pays attention	16	80	8	80
"Yes" only	8	40	5	50
Listens to all sides	3	15	1	10
Listens to one group/ substantiate own view	5	25	2	20
Doubt committee pays attention	3	15	—	—
Couldn't say	1	5	2	20
Total	20	100	10	100

The respondents were asked to estimate the impact of interest groups on the members of the committee considering their specialization measure. When the committee members "marked up" a bill in executive session, did they, in fact, pay attention to what the interest group representatives had said? An overwhelming number of congressmen (Table 17), whether or not they were members of the committee considering the specialization measure, felt that the committee members would pay attention to what the organized groups had said. Even allowing for the fact that some of the congressmen may have been responding to the question in terms of what the committees are *supposed* to do instead of in terms of what they are likely to do, the picture suggests that interest group testimony before House committees generally is given attention and consideration.

Working Interests and Peripheral Interests: A Comparison

A comparison of the congressmen's perceptions of organized groups in the area of their working interest with their perceptions in areas of peripheral interest reveals several interesting differences, if only of degree.

In general, congressmen were not contacted by large numbers of interest groups. Contacts were, nevertheless, more frequent in the areas of working interest than in peripheral areas. The visibility of interest groups to congressmen was low, on the whole, but was relatively higher in the area of working interest than in the other. In the area of a working interest, awareness of an organization's activity was normally the result of a congressman's concern with legislation. In the area of his peripheral interest, on the other hand, awareness is based on the general reputation of an organization and the public attention that its stand has received.

Some respondents would not state their own policy preferences on the peripheral issues discussed with them, and hence their perceptions of groups that agreed or disagreed with them could not be studied. Other congressmen, however, indicated their policy preferences and responded to questions about the positions of groups concerned with the issues. A characteristic of these responses was the inability of the congressmen to perceive fine shadings in the stands of interest groups in their area of peripheral interest. Groups were likely to be depicted as either being in full agreement or total disagreement with the congressmen. In the area of their working interests, on the other hand, those interviewed were able to discriminate with precision and refinement among the policy stands of various groups. In addition, they were often alert to the other interests that a group might have apart from the legislation under discussion.

There are many channels through which organized groups can contact congressmen but, in practice, most contacts are made through the mail, or by means of office calls, telephone calls, and committee hearings. When organized groups are concerned with matters not central to the congressmen's interests, they tend to restrict their contacts to a few channels and to those that are relatively formal and impersonal. Conversely, the contacts are likely to be more varied in the area of a congressman's working interest and to be less formal and impersonal.

In both areas of interest, congressmen reported few examples of frequent and continuing contact with a single group. The examples that were reported, however, were in the area of working interest. In the area of peripheral interest, the pattern was that of infrequent contacts with a few groups. As a rule, contacts are initiated by the organized group, and this is true both in the areas of working interest and peripheral interest.

Congressmen tend to accept contact with interest groups as a normal part of their job. Irritation or hostility toward these groups does not appear to be related to the congressman's working interests or peripheral interests but, instead, is associated with his attitudes toward individual organizations and the techniques that they use. Popular lore to the contrary notwithstanding, most of the respondents asserted that they did not feel pressure from organized groups either in their areas of peripheral or working interest.

Congressmen attributed at least minimal legislative importance to organized groups in the areas of both working and peripheral interest, but the bases on which they drew conclusions varied. In the first case, they relied upon first-hand observation; in the second, they placed far greater reliance on general impressions. In the area of peripheral interest, for instance, the importance attributed to organized groups was closely related to the extent of the public controversy over the issue and the attendant publicity. If the policy positions of well-known groups received wide-spread attention, congressmen were likely to attribute importance to those groups. In the absence of publicity and controversy, congressmen found it difficult to estimate the impact of organized groups on legislative behavior.

Summary

The congressman's area of specialization is also the area of specialization, as a rule, of a number of interest groups. If the congressman is particularly interested in the outcome of the legislative process in this area, so are the interest groups. At the outset, it was assumed, therefore, that the evidences of interest group activity on his specialization measure would be quite clear to a congressman and that his perceptions would be more complete and precise than in the area outside his field of specialization. In some ways these expectations were borne out, but in other ways they were not. The perceptions of the congressman concerning interest groups, even in his own specialty, remain surprisingly vague. Any single interest group contact usually makes little impression upon a congressman and does not embed itself in his memory unless it is in some way distinctive.

In his area of working interest, the congressman has more contacts than on matters outside his special field. On the whole, however, his contacts with any one interest group are not frequent. Even when a congressman has contact with a fairly large number of groups, the frequency of his contact with any one of them is likely to be slight. Close, co-operative, and enduring relationships can and do occur, but they are rare even within the range of each congressman's working interest. The congressman is not a focal point of ceaseless group activity in his area of special interest. He may feel harried, but it is rarely the pressure and activity of interest groups by themselves that produce his sense of harassment.

Congressmen agree that House committees give consideration to the testimony of interest group spokesmen. By the same token, however, consideration would also be given to the testimony of individuals who are not spokesmen of interest groups. Nothing that the respondents said suggests that testimony will be given special attention because it comes from a "lobbyist." It does not have any special merit or force because of its point of origin. In committee, the voice of any interest group is only one of several, perhaps many, voices being heard, and it must compete with these other voices for attention beyond the normal. Apparently, it is the caliber of the testimony—not its source—that will gain special consideration for the group giving it. The point is clear. The capacity of an interest group to testify before a Congressional committee does not meet the criterion of "pressure," as it is normally considered. The same is true of the information that is provided by interest group representatives. To supply information is different from applying pressure.

Interest groups rarely have the capacity to coerce legislators. They know this and the congressmen know it. Therefore, the rules of the game have been defined, informally, so as to preclude this sort of effort. Congressmen see interest groups as having a helpful and legitimate role in the legislative process, and they appear to have no quarrel with groups so long as they do not step out of that role. When this does occur and it appears to encroach on the territory of the congressman, then the reaction on the part of that individual is apt to be negative and sharp. "When a man comes in here," one congressman said, "pounds on my desk, and tries to exact a commitment from me, I'm just liable to tell him to go to hell."

How does the congressman see the two roles—the group's and his? He appears to see the role of the interest group as that of providing information, opinion, and support. The interest group may also make proposals. But the congressman feels that if it is the privilege of the interest group to propose, it is the unquestioned prerogative of the congressman to dispose. An interest group steps out of line when it attempts to tell the congressman how to make up his mind or when it tries to threaten him in any way. To do so is to confuse the support and assistance role, which is almost a staff role, with the decision-making role, which belongs solely to the congressman.

Viewing interest groups in this light, it is understandable that congressmen do not, on the whole, feel pressured by them. They attribute usefulness to them and even influence, but they do not see them as sources of "pressure."

Chapter 4

Congress and the Techniques of
Group Contacts

Each congressman interviewed was asked about the role of interest groups in connection with a measure on which he had specialized and a measure well afield from his normal area of concentration. In addition, each was asked to estimate the general effectiveness of interest groups in getting Congressional action favorable to their own areas of interest.

Importance of Groups

Over three-fourths of the congressmen (Table 18) attributed more than minimal importance to the activities of

TABLE 18. Estimated importance of organized groups in getting favorable Congressional action

Estimated Importance of Groups	Congressmen	% Congressmen
Very important	15	44
Moderately important	11	32
Not very important	4	12
Unimportant	—	—
Couldn't judge	4	12
Total	34	100

interest groups, and fifteen congressmen termed them "very important." The distribution suggests that congressmen attribute more importance to organized groups when they are speaking in general terms than when they are speaking of a specific measure.

The fifteen congressmen whose responses indicated that they considered interest groups very important qualified and explained their comments in various ways. A common observation was that an interest group was important only in its own area and on its own issue. A farm group would be listened to more carefully on farm problems than on foreign aid. Mention was made of the information-providing function of the interest groups, with the comment that, if an interest group was not well-informed concerning an issue, congressmen would pay little attention to its views. Some congressmen stated that interest groups were important because they served to focus both Congressional and public attention on an issue. They added that organized groups can build and maintain public support for a particular policy position on an issue; if a particular issue has vocal and sustained public support, Congress is more likely to take some action. Of course, during this process of building public support for a policy position on any issue, a certain amount of opposition would also develop. Consequently, the effects of any single organization may be reduced considerably. Several respondents said that while groups are important, particularly in the various services they render, the congressmen themselves are the final arbiters in making Congressional decisions.

The comments of the eleven congressmen who considered interest groups to be moderately important show a difference in emphasis from those who thought them very important. Nine volunteered comments relating primarily to the characteristics of the group involved; seven made comments relating to the issue involved; and six comments concerned the congressman himself. Most of these respondents, in other words, took more than one factor into account in making their evaluation. The congressmen who consider organized interest groups only moderately important seem to give more weight to the issue involved than do those who consider that organized groups have great importance. These congressmen also placed emphasis on the reliability of the organization, its leadership, its willingness to work with Congress, and its sophistication regarding Congressional procedure and folkways. Some of those interviewed stressed the onesidedness of interest group presentations, implying that congressmen must make allowances for the slant of the information provided by any interest group. Some congressmen placed less stress on their need for information and greater emphasis on their position as an arbiter and balancer of different points of view. Thus, when respondents placed less stress on groups as sources of information and more on group-related factors other than information, they attributed less importance to organized groups in getting favorable action.

The congressmen who characterized interest groups as having little importance in the legislative process appear to have the following perceptions in common. They have a negative orientation toward interest organizations as "pressure groups" and feel that they are not likely to be representative of their membership. Furthermore, they do not view interest groups as a source of aid and assistance to congressmen. They even place a low evaluation on these groups as reliable sources of information, often stressing that the information they provide is likely to be fragmentary and slanted.

Seniority and Party Affiliation

Since congressmen do not all see interest groups as equally important or as fulfilling the same role in Congressional action, a question arises concerning the factors that may be related to these variations in evaluation. Two factors that appear to be associated with the congressman's estimate of the importance of interest groups in legislative action are the congressman's seniority and his party affiliation.

In the present discussion, seniority in the House of Representatives is based upon the length of continuous service in the House, beginning at the time of a congressman's first *full* term of office. Table 19 gives the seniority distribution for the thirty-four congressmen who partici-

TABLE 19. Congressional seniority based on the length of continuous service in the House of Representatives[a]

Length of Continuous Service	Congressmen	% Congressmen
Low seniority	9	27
Medium seniority	11	32
High seniority	14	41
Total	34	100

a. For one analysis of the effects of the seniority system in Congress, see George Goodwin, Jr., "The Seniority System in Congress," *American Political Science Review* (June, 1959), pp. 412-36. This study suggests that the most frequent criticisms of seniority are not as accurate as some students of Congress claim. Dr. Goodwin also differentiates, as does the present study, between Congressional and committee seniority.

pated in this study, dividing them into three categories: low, medium, and high seniority. The Low seniority includes those congressmen who began their first full term of office on January 3, 1959; medium seniority includes those who began their first full term of office on January 3, 1953; and high seniority includes those who began their first first full term of office on or before January 3, 1951.

TABLE 20. Estimated importance of organized groups in getting favorable action by congressmen's seniority in House

Estimated Importance	Low Seniority	
	Congressmen	% Congressmen
Very important	8	89
Moderately important	1	11
Not very important	—	—
Unimportant	—	—
Couldn't judge	—	—
Total	9	100
	Medium Seniority	
Very important	4	37
Moderately important	3	27
Not very important	3	27
Unimportant	—	—
Couldn't judge	1	9
Total	11	100
	High Seniority	
Very important	3	21
Moderately important	7	50
Not very important	1	8
Unimportant	—	—
Couldn't judge	3	21
Total	14	100

From Table 20 it is clear that the length of continuous service in the House of Representatives is definitely related to estimates of the importance of organized interest groups. First-term members showed a decided tendency to consider organized groups very important in getting favorable action, whereas their senior colleagues took the view that organized groups had little effect on the legislative process. Of the fifteen congressmen who considered organized groups of great importance, eight were freshmen; of the eleven who considered groups of moderate importance, seven had served at least five terms in the House of Representatives. None of the freshman members, furthermore, responded that groups were of little importance or that they could not make a judgment. The evidence suggests, therefore, that the congressmen with lower seniority attribute greater importance to interest groups while the more senior members attribute less significance.

This relationship between length of continuous service in the House of Representatives and the importance attributed to organized groups is congruent with the reasons given by the congressmen for believing the groups to be important. Those who considered organized groups to be very important in the process of legislation stressed the value of the information provided by the groups, the aid given by such groups either in specific tasks or in focusing publicity on a particular issue, and the congressmen's need for such help. These functions, particularly that of providing information, may well seem more valuable to a first-term member of Congress than to his more senior colleague. Those congressmen who estimated that organized groups were moderately important in getting favorable action placed less emphasis on the information and aid given by organizations. This suggests that, as the congressmen gain experience in the House, they feel less need for the information provided by organizations, and they put increasing stress on the importance of other factors.

The standing committees of the House of Representatives, twenty in number, were placed in three categories on the basis of an estimate (the authors') of the amount and character of the contacts that each would normally have with interest groups. The first category included those standing committees with little or no committee-organized group contact; only two standing committees—Rules and House Administration—were included in this classification. The second classification included those committees that had moderate, continuous contact with organized groups; ten standing committees—Appropriations, Armed Services, Banking and Currency, District of Columbia, Foreign Affairs, Government Operations, Judiciary, Post Office and Civil Service, Science and Astronautics, Un-American Activities—were included in this classification. The third classification included those committees that have had frequent, continuing contact with organized groups and that traditionally have been centers of group controversies; eight standing committees—Agriculture, Education and Labor, Interstate and Foreign Commerce, Interior and Insular Affairs, Merchant Marine and Fisheries, Public Works, Veterans' Affairs, Ways and Means—were included in this classification. Since only one congressman was on a committee with little group contact, only the committees with moderate or frequent group contact were included.

If the congressmen assigned to these committees are classified according to committee seniority (based upon each congressman's rank position within the party listings on each committee), a pattern seems to emerge. The distribution in Table 21 shows that committee seniority makes a substantial difference in the congressmen's estimates of organized group importance in legislative action. In both of the group-committee contact classifications used, those congressmen with low committee seniority tended to attribute greater importance to organized groups than did those with high committee seniority.

The evidence in Table 21 indicates that the type of committee assignment itself is not significant in the congressmen's estimations of the importance of organized

TABLE 21. Estimated importance of organized groups in getting favorable action by congressmen's committee seniority

	Moderate Group-Committee Contact			
	Low Seniority		High Seniority	
Estimated Importance	Con-gressmen	% Con-gressmen	Con-gressmen	% Con-gressmen
Very important	7	78	3	23
Moderately important	2	22	6	47
Not very important	—	—	2	15
Unimportant	—	—	—	—
Couldn't judge	—	—	2	15
Total	9	100	13	100
	Frequent Group-Committee Contact			
Very important	4	66	1	20
Moderately important	1	17	2	40
Not very important	1	17	1	20
Unimportant	—	—	—	—
Couldn't judge	—	—	1	20
Total	6	100	5	100

groups in getting favorable action. Committee seniority is the important factor. The length of experience in working with certain organized groups and the status of the congressmen in the working situation itself seem to be the major factors.

While seniority, both within the House of Representatives and on standing committees, appears to be the most important institutional factor related to the differences in Congressional evaluations of organized group importance, the member's party affiliation also appears to have a bearing. Democratic members are more likely than Republican members to consider organized groups very important; Republican members seem more likely than Democratic members to consider organized groups either moderately important or not very important in legislative action (Table 22).

TABLE 22. Estimated importance of organized groups in getting favorable action by congressmen's party affiliation

Estimated Importance	Democrats		Republicans	
	Con-gressmen	% Con-gressmen	Con-gressmen	% Con-gressmen
Very important	11	50	4	33
Moderately important	6	27	5	42
Not very important	2	9	2	17
Unimportant	—	—	—	—
Couldn't judge	3	14	1	8
Total	22	100	12	100

Since there was no attempt to control party affiliation or length of service in Congress in drawing the Congressional sample, the party split within each House seniority classification does not necessarily reflect the partisan distribution for the entire House of Representatives. Therefore, it was necessary to obtain the partisan division by House seniority for all of the congressmen in the sample so that the effects of party affiliation could be examined more closely (Table 23).

When the figures in Table 23 are compared with those in Table 22, it appears that party affiliation has greater impact on those congressmen having low seniority than it does on those having high seniority. Of the nine congressmen with low seniority in the House of Representatives, six were Democrats and three were Republicans. All six of the low-seniority Democrats indicated that they considered organized groups very important, and two of the three Republicans so indicated. It is still not clear whether this tendency among first-term Democrats is sufficient to account for the slight "over-representation" of Democrats in the "very important" classification in Table 22; *i.e.,* the Democrats comprise 73 per cent of the very important classification but only 65 per cent of the entire sample. However, as the original sample is subdivided, with each additional step of

TABLE 23. House of Representatives seniority of all congressmen in the sample

Party Affiliation	Low Seniority Congressmen	% Congressmen
Democrat	6	67
Republican	3	33
Total	9	100
	Medium Seniority	
Democrat	9	82
Republican	2	18
Total	11	100
	High Seniority	
Democrat	7	50
Republican	7	50
Total	14	100

classification, the number of cases becomes smaller and eventually becomes statistically insignificant.

The medium- and high-seniority categories were combined, yielding a total of twenty-five congressmen who had served more than one term in the House. Of the twenty-five, sixteen were Democrats. Seven of the twenty-five estimated that organized groups were very important in legislative action; five of them (71 per cent) were Democrats. Thus, the evidence seems to suggest that Democrats, regardless of length of service in the House of Representatives, show a slightly greater tendency to estimate that organized groups are very important in getting favorable Congressional action than do the Republicans. The number of cases involved at this juncture is too small to permit confident analysis, however.

Turning to those congressmen in the "moderately important" classification, Table 22 shows that the Republicans were "over-represented"; *i.e.,* five of the eleven congressmen

(45 per cent) who considered organized groups moderately important were Republican, while Republicans comprised only 35 per cent of the sample. When the moderately important responses were divided by House seniority as well as by party affiliation, the high seniority Republicans seemed to account for this tendency. The evidence suggests, then, that the apparent Republican tendency to attribute moderate importance to organized groups stems both from party affiliation and from seniority.

That a relationship exists between party affiliation and the congressmen's estimation of the importance of organized groups is clear, but just what this relationship may be is not clear. Regardless of seniority, the Democrats seem to consider that organized interest groups are more important in getting favorable action than do Republicans. GOP members with high seniority seem more likely to attribute moderate importance to organized group action than their junior party cohorts. Democrats may attribute more importance to the activities of organized groups than the Republicans, but as the Republicans serve longer in the House of Representatives, they show a slightly greater tendency to attribute moderate importance to organized groups than do Democrats with comparable seniority. The relationship between party affiliation and the estimation of the importance of organized groups is obviously not a simple matter of the party label. Rather, the party label itself may cover differences in constituencies, in interpersonal relationships within the House of Representatives, or even differences in types of personality. In this realm, however, the number of examples involved is too small at present to provide a basis for more than conjecture.

Effectiveness of Various Techniques

The importance that congressmen attribute to interest groups should be related to their estimate of the effectiveness of the various contact techniques. Therefore, a broad examination of Congressional perceptions of interest group activities must include the reactions of congressmen to the individual techniques used by interest groups. The congressmen were asked to estimate the effectiveness of each of thirteen separate techniques used by organizations and by individuals to contact members of Congress. The techniques were: individual letters, form letters, petitions, telegrams, telephone calls, office calls, committee hearings, contact through a friend, contact through conversation with a constituent, social engagements, invitations to speak at organization meetings, campaign work, campaign contributions. The congressmen were simply asked to estimate the effectiveness of various techniques, and no attempt was made to establish a rank order of effectiveness of the techniques.[1]

For purposes of analysis, the thirteen techniques were divided into four major types: indirect personal contacts (Table 24), direct personal contacts (Table 25), collective personal contacts (Table 26), campaign contacts (Table 27). These tables show the distribution of the congressmen's estimate of the effectiveness of all thirteen specific contact techniques broken down into these four categories.

The congressmen themselves made a distinction between the effectiveness of these techniques when used by organized groups and by individuals. It was clear that the effectiveness of some of these techniques depended to a certain extent on the appropriateness of the technique to the person or persons using it. If he considers that a contact comes from

1. See Lester W. Milbrath, "Lobbying as a Communication Process," *The Public Opinion Quarterly*, 24 (Spring, 1960), 32-53. Milbrath asked his respondents to rank order a variety of techniques and was able, therefore, to make more precise comparisons in the estimations of effectiveness of the contact techniques than was possible in the method of questioning used in the present study. However, Milbrath concentrates primarily on lobbyist attitudes and estimations of the effectiveness of a variety of techniques, and his list of techniques was, apparently, somewhat different from the list used in this study.

the wrong source or if it is not used for the correct purpose associated with it, a congressman will downgrade the effectiveness of the technique for achieving legislative goals.

Generally speaking, the indirect and direct personal contact techniques were considered most effective in getting favorable Congressional action. The collective personal contact techniques and campaign contacts were considered either ineffective or minimally effective. Giving a party or making a campaign contribution, therefore, does not necessarily promote favorable legislative action—a fact that serious students of Congress have long known.

To discover the bases used in evaluating particular techniques, the comments volunteered by the congressmen were examined to see if recurrent themes were associated with individual techniques. Table 24, for example, indicates that those interviewed believe personal letters to be effective in achieving Congressional action. They likewise believe that letters are given far more weight if they appear to be the expression of individual views rather than the product of interest group stimulation. Letters that are well-reasoned and factual are likely to receive special attention, since they indicate that the writer knows his subject. "A letter that tells me the writer's point of view and that gives facts and explains the writer's reasoning is a real help," one congressman said. "A letter that insults me or just demands that I do something, or that asks when we lunkheads are going to do something about this or that doesn't help at all. A letter like that has no real influence."

On the whole, congressmen did not regard stimulated mail as an effective technique for interest group use. One congressman expressed himself at length on the subject: "I get a lot of stereotyped letters. That's bad enough, but in addition the letters haven't got the facts right. These people haven't read the bill and don't understand it. They get orders from their Chamber of Commerce secretary to 'write their

TABLE 24. Estimated effectiveness of selected indirect personal contact techniques in getting favorable Congressional action

Estimated Effectiveness	Individual Letters Congressmen	% Congressmen
Very effective	10	30
Moderately effective	8	23
Not very effective	3	9
Not effective	—	—
Can be effective	12	35
Don't know	1	3
Total	**34**	**100**
Form Letters		
Very effective	—	—
Moderately effective	1	3
Not very effective	11	32
Not effective	16	47
Can be effective	6	18
Don't know	—	—
Total	**34**	**100**
Petitions		
Very effective	—	—
Moderately effective	1	3
Not very effective	9	26
Not effective	13	38
Can be effective	11	32
Don't know	—	—
Total	**34**	**99a**
Telegrams		
Very effective	1	3
Moderately effective	4	12
Not very effective	7	21
Not effective	5	14
Can be effective	14	41
Don't know	3	9
Total	**34**	**100**
Telephone Calls		
Very effective	5	14
Moderately effective	6	18
Not very effective	6	18
Not effective	1	3
Can be effective	11	32
Don't know	5	14
Total	**34**	**99a**

a. Totals do not equal 100 per cent because of rounding errors.

Congressman' and they are told what to say. But the Chamber of Commerce people themselves haven't read the bill and so I get a desk full of letters that are all the same and all wrong."

When groups did instigate a mail campaign, congressmen would treat the letters much as if they were form letters, placing a low estimate on their value. As Table 24 shows, form letters were not considered very effective in producing favorable Congressional action. Almost half of the congressmen rejected the idea that form letters were given serious consideration, and many of them expressed irritation when they were used extensively. "I answer them," one congressman commented, "but I don't like them." One congressman did say, nevertheless, that he felt pressure when he received a large volume of mail, even if he knew it to be stimulated, because it made him feel that "the eyes of the people are upon me."

The respondents indicated that they had little trouble in spotting stimulated mail. The process was explained as follows: If the mail on a given question suddenly increases, the letters are watched for the repetition of a single argument or several sets of arguments. If a pattern emerges, the letters are treated as form letters even when they appear to be from individuals.

One midwestern congressman told about his experience with such mail on the St. Lawrence Seaway project. He had already decided to vote against it because he thought it would mean higher transportation costs for products shipped out of his district. Suddenly, he began to get a lot of letters from the district urging him to support it. They were all nice letters, and they were all obviously handwritten by the persons who had signed them. Some letters even contained grammatical errors and misspelled words. They were written on various kinds of stationery with all kinds of pens and ink, but they all contained one of three or four sets of arguments. Moreover, he would get a batch from around one town at one time, and then a few days later another batch from another town. When they first started coming in, he had thought that they were genuine expressions of individual opinion, but as he got more of them and the pattern emerged, he knew they were stimulated. They were not going to change his own position, but he did wonder who was backing this mail campaign.

One day the congressman got one of these letters from Old Joe. Now, he had known Old Joe for over twenty years, and he knew Old Joe didn't know anything about the St. Lawrence Seaway—probably didn't even know where the St. Lawrence was. He had a few things to talk over with Old Joe, so he called him up. They chatted for a few moments, and during the course of the conversation, he casually asked who was going around to all those meetings in the district asking people to write in about the St. Lawrence Seaway. Old Joe said it was a farmer from upstate New York and gave his name. When the congressman heard the name, he knew right away what was happening, and he told Old Joe that this was no New York farmer but a $75,000-a-year lobbyist for Hanna Steel. It turned out that the lobbyist had been going around to all of these meetings and urging people to write to the congressman. He had even provided them with several lists of arguments and a variety of stationery, pens, and ink so they could sit down and write before they left the meeting. The congressman laughed and said that some of these lobbyists would do the darnedest things sometimes to try to fool you, and he had joked with this particular lobbyist about it the next time he saw him.

The general reaction of the congressmen to the use of petitions was approximately the same as their reaction to form letters. Petitions are more obviously the product of organized effort than are form letters, so there is even less tendency to consider the result an expression of the signer's real concern. The congressmen indicated that petitions were not very effective since it was never hard to collect signatures. Several cited instances in which a constituent had written asking them to disregard his signature on a petition since he had signed it rather than refuse a friend.

One congressman described how he had learned his lesson concerning petitions. Some years ago he had received a petition urging him to vote against vivisection. One name on the petition caught his eye—it was his son's name. That night he asked the boy why he had signed the petition. His son answered, "I didn't even know what vivisection was, but a friend asked me to sign and so I did."

Another congressman said he used to try to write a letter to each person who signed a petition, but he gave it up when he kept getting replies from these people asking what petition he was talking about. Some of the respondents explained that they use form letters and petitions for reverse propaganda—they write the signers of such letters and petitions and present their own point of view. Several congressmen stated that petitions could be minimally effective if received in sufficient volume, since they indicated that many people knew about the issue even if their signatures did not necessarily prove very deep convictions.

Telegrams, as a means of contact, bear some of the same characteristics as form letters and petitions, and congressmen tend to group these three together when considering their effectiveness. Frequent mention was made of the lack of effort required on the part of the sender, the ease of persuading people to send telegrams, and the ease with which false names can be used. Those who felt that telegrams could have an influence emphasized that much depended on the content of a telegram and whether its sender was known to the congressman.

By and large, the respondents indicate that the central factor in indirect personal contacts—stimulated mail, petitions, telegrams, and telephone calls—is whether they represent an expression of genuine personal opinion, particularly opinion from the district. Since it is hard for an interest group to use these contact techniques while maintaining the personal touch, this means that these techniques are limited in the effect they can have on the congressmen. They can even boomerang and achieve a result opposite to the group's intent.

Examination of the comments most often made concerning direct personal contact reveals an even greater emphasis on the personal element. Many congressmen indicated that they preferred this type of contact to mail, petitions, telegrams, and telephone calls because it offers a chance for a face-to-face meeting and for mutual exchange of views. However, the distribution in Table 25 suggests that their preference is not based solely upon the personal element in face-to-face meetings. To the personal element must be added the appropriateness and legitimacy of using these techniques in approaching the congressmen.

The office call is an example of direct personal contact, and almost half (sixteen) of the thirty-four congressmen expressed the opinion that they considered office calls either moderately effective or very effective in getting favorable action. Eleven other congressmen said that they felt office calls could be important. Eleven of those interviewed—not the same eleven—qualified their estimate of the importance of office calls by saying that their effectiveness depended on who the caller was and whether he was known to the congressman or was a constituent. Some respondents said explicitly that office calls from paid representatives of organized groups are less effective than calls from friends or constituents.

Testifying at committee hearings was considered the single most effective of all thirteen techniques. It was particularly effective as a vehicle for organized groups in getting

TABLE 25. Estimated effectiveness of selected direct personal contact techniques in getting favorable Congressional action

Estimated Effectiveness	Office Call	
	Congressmen	% Congressmen
Very effective	8	23
Moderately effective	8	23
Not very effective	3	9
Not effective	1	3
Can be effective	11	32
Don't know	3	9
Total	34	99a
	Committee Hearing	
Very effective	18	53
Moderately effective	6	18
Not very effective	1	3
Not effective	—	—
Can be effective	8	23
Don't know	1	3
Total	34	100
	Through a Personal Friend	
Very effective	4	12
Moderately effective	6	18
Not very effective	8	23
Not effective	4	12
Can be effective	8	23
Don't know	4	12
Total	34	100
	Conversation with Constituent	
Very effective	4	12
Moderately effective	7	21
Not very effective	8	23
Not effective	5	14
Can be effective	7	21
Don't know	3	9
Total	34	100

a. Totals do not equal 100 per cent because of rounding errors.

action favorable to them. Table 25 indicates that eighteen congressmen consider committee testimony very effective in legislative action, and six consider it moderately effective. Thus, twenty-four of the thirty-four congressmen thought that committee testimony was more than minimally effective in getting favorable action from Congress.

Several of those questioned emphasized that much depended on the witness—how well he was prepared, how much confidence the committee members had in him, and who he was. "You take Jimmy Hoffa," one congressman said. "He didn't do himself any good before Congressional committees. He would have done better to stay home." No congressman regarded committee testimony as completely ineffective.

The congressmen's responses to committee hearings indicated that they regard hearings as a forum where they receive factual information on the matter before them, and where they may weigh and consider opposing arguments. It is the occasion on which those who have a special point of view or who have done research on an issue can meet with the congressmen. Even those congressmen who were skeptical of the value of much of the testimony they listened to conceded that, on the whole, committee hearings are valuable and help committee members in their deliberations.

The congressmen's comments indicated that the committee hearing is part of the established, formal Congressional procedure and is the proper forum in which all interested parties should present their cause. The committee hearing sets the scene for legislative conflict with the committee member as mediator or, sometimes, as advocate for one position. The respondents consider this *the* most appropriate forum before which interest groups should plead their case. However, not all participants in this process share the congressmen's enthusiasm for the effectiveness of committee testimony. Milbrath's study of the Washington lobbyists shows that the lobbyists rated the personal presentation of argument above testifying at hearings.[2]

The other two direct personal contact techniques—introduction to a congressman by a personal friend or by a constituent—are rated by the congressmen as approximately equal in legislative effectiveness (Table 25). Congressmen who rated these contact techniques high on the scale of effectiveness were usually those who emphasized the importance of the personal factor in contacts. Conversely, as might have been expected, those who did not place a very high evaluation on personal contact gave a low rating to personal contact techniques. Over half of those interviewed doubted that either of the above techniques would be useful in approaching them. They appeared to feel that, if anyone wanted to see them, a direct contact could be made with ease and that nothing significant was gained by an introduction through a friend or a constituent. In the latter case, they might listen a bit longer, but that was all.

Popular lore concerning interest group relations with Congress devotes a good deal of attention to the importance of giving congressmen a good time at parties. Presumably, these affairs place a congressman under obligation to the host organization, and he, in gratitude, grants whatever the organization requests. Serious students of Congress, however, have maintained that invitations to social gatherings have little or no effect on a congressman's attitude toward an organization. The data in Table 26 bear out this contention. In the judgment of the respondents, gatherings give a congressman an opportunity to meet the members of an organization—and that is all. By themselves, the figures in Table 26, unfortunately, do not convey the vehemence with which many of the respondents rejected the possibility that social engagements had a significant effect on legislation. Most of the respondents who commented on social gatherings

2. *Ibid.*

TABLE 26. Estimated effectiveness of selected collective personal contact techniques in getting favorable Congressional action

Estimated Effectiveness	Social Engagements		Speak at Organization Meetings	
	Congressmen	% Congressmen	Congressmen	% Congressmen
Very effective	—	—	—	—
Moderately effective	1	3	3	9
Not very effective	9	26	4	12
Not effective	17	50	13	38
Can be effective	4	12	3	9
Don't know	3	9	11	32
Total	34	100	34	100

at all said that they considered such engagements to be irritating, harassing, and a waste of time. They attended as few as possible, went only out of a sense of duty, and did not leave these functions with a friendly feeling toward the sponsoring organization. The few congressmen who said that social gatherings could be important explained that it depended on who attended. If the right people were there, it could not hurt and might even help get some action on legislation. But even these men indicated that parties were sources of boredom and irritation more often than not.

Many congressmen seemed doubtful about the value—both to the congressman and to the group—of invitations to speak to meetings of group members. Those who commented on this technique considered it to be about as effective as social gatherings. Speeches of this kind were seen as requiring the congressmen's time and effort, while yielding little return to the group. Some of the respondents said they accepted such invitations primarily when they wanted to have an opportunity to put across to an audience their own views or when they felt that they should out of a sense of duty. There was agreement that contacts of this kind could hardly affect a congressman's vote on legislative matters.

The popular literature would have it that if an interest group helps a congressman get elected, it more or less owns him from that point on. How does the congressman feel about this? Does he feel that accepting a campaign contribution from an interest group or accepting its help in a campaign places him under heavy obligation?

TABLE 27. Estimated effectiveness of selected campaign contact techniques in getting favorable Congressional action

Estimated Effectiveness	Campaign Work		Campaign Contribution	
	Congressmen	% Congressmen	Congressmen	% Congressmen
Very effective	2	6	2	6
Moderately effective	5	14	4	12
Not very effective	6	18	5	14
Not effective	6	18	11	32
Can be effective	7	21	6	18
Don't know	8	23	6	18
Total	34	100	34	100

Table 27 indicates that congressmen generally do not view either of these techniques as very effective when they are used by interest groups. Those respondents who felt that working in a campaign would be a moderately effective technique said that it would probably engender a friendlier feeling on their part toward the group. They made it clear, however, that campaign activity by an interest group should be interpreted as support for the candidate rather than an attempt to get the candidate to support the group.

Those congressmen who minimized the importance of campaign activity remarked that while spokesmen for an organization might say that the organization would work for him (or, far more rarely, against him), the organization was rarely able to deliver. The reason for this, it was suggested, is that organizations do not have the machinery to work in the field for a congressman, often do not have the resources, and are rarely sufficiently concerned about an individual candidate to make a significant effort for or against him.

There was a high degree of agreement that campaign contributions are not very effective in influencing the legislative process. One congressman made the point by saying, "While you don't kick your contributors in the face, neither do you have to do everything they tell you." A large percentage of those questioned took an emphatic stand, rejecting with vehemence the suggestion that campaign contributions had any effect on legislative action. Most of them said they had never had a contributor ask them for anything, and some of them cited instances in which they had voted contrary to the interests of contributors. One congressman spoke of a recent letter in which a contributor said that he still liked the congressman and still wanted to help keep him in office, even though he often took exception to the way the congressman voted. The congressman commented that he liked to get that kind of letter. A number of respondents stated that they did not like the idea of receiving contributions from interest groups, and others said flatly that they would not accept them. Some congressmen admitted that they did not know who contributed to their campaign and preferred not to know.

Summary

By and large, congressmen attribute more than minimal importance to interest groups, and almost half of those interviewed said they thought the groups were very important. At the same time, most congressmen felt that the impact of any one organization rarely extended beyond its special sphere of interest. The AMA, a force to reckon with on public health questions, would have little, if any, leverage on farm legislation.

Variations in the effectiveness attributed to interest groups by congressmen appear to be associated with seniority and party affiliation. The more senior congressmen attribute less influence to interest groups than do the more junior members. Likewise, there is some evidence that Democrats attribute greater influence to interest groups than do Republicans. The explanation of variations in the importance attributed to groups, however, is no doubt complex and depends on other factors, such as the special experience of individual congressmen, their personalities, and their ideas on the legislative process.

The importance that congressmen attribute to interest groups should be associated with their evaluation of the effectiveness of the various contact techniques used by these groups. Interestingly, there is an apparent disjuncture between the high level of influence that congressmen attribute to the role of pressure groups in general and the relatively low ratings they give the individual contact techniques. Their detailed responses, that is, do not seem to bear out their broader pronouncements. A partial explanation for the disparity may be that when the congressmen were asked to evaluate the *effectiveness* of interest groups, they did not respond to that question but instead responded as though they were asked whether they thought interest groups played an important role in the American governmental system. This helps explain a relationship noted in the data—the more importance that congressmen attributed to the gaining of information, the more highly were they likely to rate the effectiveness of interest groups. In short, the importance of the role that interest groups play in the legislative process involves one set of considerations, while the actual effectiveness of the various techniques involves a quite different set. A congressman might, therefore, term interest groups "important" in the first sense, while yet attributing relatively little effectiveness to the various contact techniques.

In addition, congressmen appear to think of interest groups in more stereotyped terms the more general the question asked regarding them. The more immediate their observation of these groups, the more precise and detailed would be their comments. The more general the question, the more likely the congressman is to respond unreflectively in terms of the ongoing ideology concerning interest groups.

In querying congressmen about individual contact techniques, it became clear that the personal element is an important ingredient in the successful use of any technique. Personal contact, by itself, does not guarantee success, to be sure, as witness the preponderant agreement among congressmen that social engagements have very little value.

Chapter 5

Congressmen and Interest Groups

An Altered Perspective

To do its job well, Congress must have means for taking into account the wants and needs of various elements within the United States. Interest groups help register these wants and needs; therefore, their position is both respectable and assured. There is a popular point of view, however, that is not content to see interest groups as simply one of several influences working on the legislative process but prefers to regard them as dominating that process. For this interpretation of their role to be valid, several important conditions would have to be realized.

1. Organized interest groups would need to have a virtual monopoly of access to Congress and congressmen;

2. Interest groups would need effective instruments at their disposal by means of which they could exert pressure on congressmen;

3. Congress, as a whole, would have to be fundamentally passive and to be highly susceptible to interest group pressure. The same would, of course, have to be true of many congressmen.

In considering the first of these conditions, it must be noted that interest groups do not have a virtual monopoly of access to congressmen. A congressman will normally talk to many individuals other than interest group representatives and read a great deal of material from non-interest group sources. The views of constituents, friends, the party leadership, the House leadership, committee chairman, and committee colleagues may have a bearing on his vote. If the congressman belongs to the same party as the President, the preferences of the President will carry weight with him. One congressman made the point very clearly: "Now, of course, if you are a member of the Administration party, then you try to get the viewpoint of the President. You have to know whether something under consideration is in line with the President's program and with what the Bureau of the Budget sends up. That's the first thing to find out."

The second condition mentioned above raises the question of whether interest groups have techniques at their disposal capable of exerting significant pressure on congressmen. A key instrument of power would be the capacity of an interest group to defeat a congressman at the polls. It is generally agreed that this instrument is rarely at the lobbyists's disposal.[1] One congressman made the point in his interview: "Interest groups don't bother me much. I

1. See, for example, David Truman, *The Governmental Process* (New York: Alfred A. Knopf, Inc., 1958), p. 314.

tell them where I stand on an issue. If they agree—fine. If they don't, I tell them they can always go to my district and try to get a majority of the voters on their side. No one has tried yet."

The data presented in this study have shown that the potency of most contact techniques used by interest groups is slight. The instruments that might be important are illegal (bribery), suspect (making a campaign contribution), or impractical (trying to influence a congressman's election). Little of significance is left save office calls and testimony before Congressional committees.

The function performed by interest groups that is most highly rated by congressmen is that of providing information. As a basis of power, however, the information function leaves much to be desired.

> As a source of power, the willingness of a group to provide helpful services, such as information and research, does not count for much. However, such nonthreatening acts as serving as a source of expert knowledge become much more crucial when the vague notion of power is put aside and the legislator is asked to give his reasons for listening to the claims of a particular group; "pressure groups are most welcome in the legislative arena when they go beyond a mere assertion of demands and interests and present information and data which help legislators work out compromises and adjustments among the most insistent demands of groups on the basis of some vague conception of the public interest against which particular claims can be judged." Legislators do not like to be "pressured," and, while they operate upon the assumption that interest groups are powerful, they react to specific group claims more on the basis of usefulness.[2]

2. Harmon Zeigler, *Interest Groups in American Society* (Englewood Cliffs, New Jersey: Prentice-Hall, 1964), pp. 270-71. Zeigler is quoting from Walke *et al.*, *The Legislative System* (New York: John Wiley & Sons, 1962), pp. 338-39.

One reason that the information function does not give the interest group greater leverage is that the group does not have an information monopoly. There is normally a variety of alternative sources that the congressman can take advantage of if he is energetic and if his need is great enough. Information offered to the congressman by an interest group must often compete for his attention with information coming from other sources—newspapers, magazines, Executive Branch documents, Legislative Reference Service products, and so on. It is one thing to provide a congressman with information in competition with other sources, and it is quite another thing to be able to influence his vote in a significant way.

From the point of view of the interest group, the problem is that it rarely has anything to give or withhold that is of more than marginal significance to the congressman. Its bargaining position is inherently weak since the instruments available to it are not the stuff out of which "pressure" can be fashioned. One congressman, who had spent more than three and a half decades in the House, argued that lobbyists now conduct themselves in a more gentlemanly and restrained fashion than they once did. "Lobbyists are now friendly and courteous," he remarked, "and never threaten and demand." He went on to add that he never felt pressured by them. One reason that lobbyists are rarely demanding is that they are seldom in a position to back up their demands. If they are more mannerly now than previously, it may be associated with declining power.

The group interpretation of legislative behavior offers an elite theory of government. Like most elite theories, it places heavy demands on the alleged elite. Unfortunately for the theory, interest groups cannot live up to their billing; they simply do not have the instruments of power at their disposal. This shortcoming is of critical importance for the group approach. The mechanism that is supposed to connect the interest group, on the one hand, and Congress, on the other, is the "pressure" that the interest group is presumed to be able to exert on Congress by various means. If the instruments in the hands of lobbyists are weak, therefore, there is no basis for a coercive relationship, or even a bargaining one, and an element essential to the theory has been removed.

Interest groups are miscast when given the central role in the American political system. It is significant that the lobbyists themselves appear to agree that lobbying is often of marginal importance to the over-all policy process. Lester Milbrath asked his lobbyist respondents to rank, in relative importance for policy-making, the following influences: lobbying, President, Congress, executive agencies, political parties, opinion leaders, and voters.

> Most important for our purposes, only one lobbyist gives first rank importance to lobbying, and only five rate it second. Congressional respondents also accord very slight importance to lobbying in making public policy; about half of them, in fact, place lobbying at the bottom of the list. It is rather striking that both the practitioners and the recipients of lobbying think that lobbying is of so little importance in making public policy. One lobbyist struggling with this question said: "I don't know where in the world I would fit the lobbyists as a group. Some of them have been up here for years battling for lost causes. On the whole, and speaking of all lobbyists in general, I think they are a lot less effective than most people believe."[3]

The third condition noted above involves the question of whether Congress is fundamentally passive and highly susceptible to interest group pressures. To maintain that it is, is to underestimate the extent to which the institutional defenses of Congress allow it to control the play of group

3. Lester Milbrath, *The Washington Lobbyists* (Chicago: Rand McNally, 1963), p. 352.

activities within its walls. Congress does not receive these "pressures" passively but actively molds and channels them. The working of the House of Representatives is governed by a set of rules, both formal and informal. These rules provide the framework within which interest groups must operate, if they are to operate at all. For example, if congressmen react negatively to certain approaches and the use of certain contact techniques, interest groups will avoid their use. The ability of Congress to define informally the types of interest group activity that are acceptable and those that are not makes it more the arbiter of group activities than its helpless victim. This can be seen in connection with the information function performed by interest groups.

The primary justification of interest groups in the eyes of many congressmen appears to be that they serve as vehicles for conveying information and opinion from various segments of the public to the congressmen. They perform a middleman's function or a broker's function. If this is the activity that gives them legitimacy and importance, it is also the basis on which they can be judged. If an interest group is not normally successful in providing congressmen with needed information and analysis, its standing with them will suffer. By the same token, those techniques that do not facilitate the flow of information are likely to be deemed ineffective. Since making a campaign contribution or participating in a campaign does not contribute to the information function of interest groups, these techniques get low marks in this respect.

The attitude that some congressmen have toward these particular techniques is not explained solely by their irrelevance to the information process, nevertheless. The difficulty appears to be that these techniques carry with them the tacit implication that the interest group using them is trying to bind the congressman in some way. The congressman tends to believe that interest groups exist, as far as he is concerned, to perform certain service functions that are primarily information-related. He feels that he is not much more obligated to a group when he avails himself of its information facilities than he would be to the information clerk at National Airport. The problem with financial and other contributions to a campaign is that it is difficult for the congressman to remain free of obligation to those who helped him. If he accepts assistance of this kind, he is placed in a position where he must either appear to be an ingrate or he must labor under some sense of obligation; therefore, he may refuse this kind of assistance. Alternatively, he may make it clear to the interest group beforehand that, whatever it does for him, he is determined, as a matter of principle, to be ungrateful for its help. Of course, if the congressman's views are virtually identical to those of the interest group, he would feel no constraint in any case and therefore would welcome interest group support.

Congressmen customarily resent any suggestion that they are in bondage to interest groups, and they are made uneasy by interest group actions that appear to carry with them the tacit implication that a congressman *should* feel some sense of obligation in return for services rendered. In the eyes of many a congressman, an interest group commits a cardinal sin when it tries to impinge upon what he conceives to be his rightful prerogatives. The use of non-information techniques by an interest group is open to the interpretation that the group is trying to move out of its proper sphere of responsibility (information, analysis, representation) and into the congressman's sphere of responsibility (decision-making) by efforts to curtail his freedom of decision.

The emphasis that many congressmen place on the information function performed by interest groups should be interpreted, at least in part, as a symptom of failure on the part of Congress. Virtually every large organization encounters problems in gathering, storing, and using information, and Congress is no exception. Indeed, its information needs are disproportionately great for its size since it is expected to legislate, with knowledge and understanding, on a bewildering variety of topics. The problem is further complicated because the professional background and training of many congressmen do not equip them to deal with the technical aspects of many issues with which they are confronted. One of the reasons that congressmen place a high value on the information provided by interest groups is that Congress itself does not provide adequate alternative ways to satisfy information needs. Despite the vital importance of information to the proper functioning of Congress, that body has not assessed its information requirements and attempted to meet them.

The evidence of this study points toward a need for reexamination and reorganization of Congressional arrangements for gathering, processing, retrieving, analyzing, and using information. Those who are troubled by the presumed power of interest groups might consider whether this feature of Congressional reform would not do more to weaken the position of interest groups than passage of more stringent lobby registration requirements. Removing the basis for a key service function performed by interest groups might be a more effective way of dealing with interest groups than the use of legislation. The real case to be made against the information-providing role of interest groups, however, is not so much that it strengthens those groups as that it prompts congressmen to rely upon informal, inadequate, unsystematic, hit-or-miss, self-serving sources of information.

Just as Congress as a whole has defenses against interest groups, however, so has the individual congressman. He is often conscious of occupying a position of importance and one that confers a good deal of status. He is likely to have distinct ideas about the deference and respect that are due him as a congressman, and behavior that trespasses on his sense of personal worth or that indicates a lack of respect for his position touches a sensitive nerve. When a spokesman for an interest group oversteps himself in dealing with a congressman, he runs the dual risk of affronting the congressman's ideas about the manner in which an interest group should conduct itself and offending his sense of dignity and integrity. Lobbyists are normally sensitive to the expectations of congressmen, for to be unaware of them or to ignore them would doom a lobbyist to ineffectiveness.

During the interviews, the respondents frequently remarked that groups ceased to bother them once their personal position had been made clear. If a lobbyist should be persistent, a congressman can refuse to see him or can listen to him and go on to vote as he had planned to. One congressman made the point in the following way: "When a man takes a job like this he has to expect that people are going to be getting in touch with him. If that makes him nervous he ought not to be here. A man that doesn't like heat should get out of the kitchen. These people come to see me but I don't regard it as pressure. I know that when they walk out of my office I'm just as free to vote the way I want as I was before they walked in."

The evidence presented in this study suggests that congressmen have substantially more freedom of action vis-à-vis interest groups than is commonly understood. In addition to group contacts, many other stimuli impinge upon a congressman, and any of them may be decisive in one case and of negligible importance in another. The personal outlook of a congressman is often a vital factor in influencing his vote; he, like other men (and more than most men), will have policy preferences, and he has ample opportunity to give them play. Day in and day out a congressman casts votes on matters in which his decisions are indeterminate insofar as external forces are concerned. This indeterminacy may be resolved by a colleague's comment as he enters the chamber or even by something that is said on the floor. The situation has been described elsewhere: "On most important bills there are usually a number of members who are not able to make up their minds how to vote until the last minute. When the floor amendments raise puzzling new questions and cut members adrift from past commitments, this number may be quite large. Under such circumstances a well-oriented speech or series of speeches can often directly influence fence sitters to jump in one direction or another."[4]

To be sure, there are issues on which the vote of a congressman may be highly predictable. Congressmen from the deep South have little freedom of action on civil rights matters, as a rule, and farm-state representatives are likely to toe the mark when farm legislation relating to products from their districts is being voted upon. The examples that come to mind usually involve constituent needs and preferences, however, rather than those of interest groups as such. A congressman might come from a district in which an interest group, say the American Medical Association, was well entrenched; therefore, he might find it politic to vote in accordance with the preferences of the AMA on matters central to its interests. The point to keep in mind, however, is that the congressman might have a high degree of freedom of action in all *other* areas. If his votes were foreordained on 3 per cent of the bills on which he acted, he would still have freedom of action on the other 97 per cent. Perspective on this point is hard to retain, nevertheless, and the predilections of observers lead them to give far more attention to the 3 per cent than to the 97.

Another point of importance is that the area of freedom of action varies from congressman to congressman. If Congressman A listens when the Fruitgrowers Association speaks, Congressmen B, C, D, E, and F are indifferent to

4. Bertram M. Gross, *The Legislative Struggle: A Study in Social Combat* (New York: McGraw-Hill, 1953), pp. 366-67.

the pleas of the association. Congressman B, in turn, might be vulnerable to a second group to which his colleagues A, C, D, E, and F are indifferent. When the patterns of individual vulnerability are overlaid on one another, so to speak, it is clear that relatively few congressmen are vulnerable to any given group. Individual vulnerabilities cancel each other out to a considerable extent and are lost in the indifference, inertia, and invulnerability of Congress as a whole. Advocates of the group interpretation of politics are led astray in dealing with Congress because they do not allow for this canceling-out process, instead, and, assume that Congress is a single, vulnerable congressman writ large.

Each of the three conditions associated with the group interpretation that were mentioned at the beginning of the chapter must be rejected as oversimple. It is not surprising, then, that the behavioral consequences implied by the theory are not to be found. If interest groups rarely have the capacity to exert "pressure" on congressmen in the sense of coercing them, these groups may, nevertheless, exercise a degree of influence in a roundabout way. It was noted earlier that well-known interest groups advocating generally recognized positions are deemed by congressmen to be more important than less well-known groups. This means that an effective public relations campaign might be valuable to a group if it succeeded in creating public support for itself, the interests it speaks for, and the measures it is supporting. There are indications that interest groups have recognized the relative ineffectiveness of direct approaches to congressmen and have been devoting an increasing proportion of their energies and resources in recent years to the indirect approach.[5] This process involves an impact on the public first, however, and only indirectly—through constituents or the press—on the congressman. It is, therefore, a quite different process from lobbying, and it has not been

5. See Zeigler, *Interest Groups*, p. 233.

the basis on which advocates of the group interpretation have argued the potency of interest groups.

If the influence of interest groups on Congress must be downgraded, then the capacity of this body to act in relative independence of interest groups must be correspondingly upgraded. One of the reasons that the image of the congressman has been so tarnished in the United States is the widespread folk belief that he is a tool of "the interests." Once interest groups cease to be regarded as all-powerful, however, congressmen no longer need to be viewed as their puppets. If interest groups are reduced to life size, furthermore, the simplistic, mechanical view of the legislative process is undermined. Instead of interpreting legislative action solely in the light of interest group pressures on the legislature, it becomes possible to see legislators as actors in their own right, having policy preferences of their own.

This view of the legislative process also makes it clear that, if legislative action is *not* simply the vector of interest group pressures on Congress, there must be room for concern on the part of the legislators for the national interest. "Many who would not deny to doctors and lawyers the possibility of a concern for their patients and clients, to teachers a concern for their students, and to workmen an effort to do well what is expected of them, nevertheless find it hard to concede the possibility that legislators may sometimes be animated by a concern for the national welfare."[6]

To suggest that congressmen may have a concern for the public interest is not to say that a "national interest" necessarily exists, in the sense that a supremely wise and disinterested observer could point to it, or that all congressmen will agree on the policies that will best advance the public interest. The point is simply that congressmen can and do have ideas relating to the welfare of the nation as a whole,

6. Andrew M. Scott, *Political Thought in America* (New York: Holt, Rinehart and Winston, Inc., 1959), p. 517.

that these ideas are not defined wholly in terms of group advantage, that congressmen have an opportunity to introduce these ideas in Congress and, lastly, that congressmen often have freedom of action to vote as they think best on such questions exempt from inordinate interest group pressures. Failure to understand this point does an injustice to a great many congressmen and stands in the way of a real understanding of the legislative process.[7]

It is doubtful that the oversimplifications associated with the group approach to the study of Congress can long survive in an era in which researchers rely less on a priori truths than formerly and more on careful observation of political processes. If the long-term survival prospects of the group approach must be regarded as dim in a behavioral era, the contributions of that approach to the study of politics and of Congressional activity must not be overlooked. Though tending toward dogmatism and sectarianism, the approach has alerted scholars to an aspect of political reality that might not otherwise have received its due. If it is soon to be replaced by a more flexible approach to the study of groups in the political process, its historical role has, nevertheless, been important.

7. "Group theorists, like the early radical behaviorists, have all but banished reason, knowledge, and intelligence from the governmental process. Public policy and administration are regarded as vectors of group pressures—a kind of resultant in a parallelogram of group forces. . . . Decision-makers are regarded either as neutrals pushed this way or that by the group pressures that impinge upon them, or as active group partisans whose own group interests determine their decisions. The notion of the decision-maker as a rational creature motivated by considerations of the 'general welfare' or the 'public interest,' making his decisions in the light of logic and the weight of the evidence, is regarded as a naïve residue of the romantic Heavenly City of the eighteenth-century philosophers.

"My concern about this line of argument is that the group theorists, in their quite reasonable rejection of rationality as the sole or major factor in political decision-making have all but banished rationality from the governmental process." Peter H. Odegard, "A Group Basis of Politics: A New Name for an Ancient Myth," *The Western Political Quarterly*, XI (1958), 699.

Appendix

I am doing research on a phase of the relationship between congressmen and organized interest groups—not only organized lobbies, but organized groups throughout the country that may be interested in legislation. I would like to talk to you about your own personal experiences with organized interest groups in a legislative area with which you are familiar and also in one with which you have not been actively associated.

1. Concerning legislation with which you have had personal experience during this session, on what bill have you done the most work? _____

---

2. Could you tell me something about its background?_____

   a. Why did you become interested in this bill?_____

   b. What action have you taken regarding this bill?_____

   c. How far along is the bill now?_____

3. What contact have you had with organized interest groups regarding this legislation? _____

   What were the names of some of these groups? _____

   (If respondent names more than three groups, ask:) _____

   Which ones of these would you consider were the three most important? _____

   (Ask only concerning these three groups.)

G1: _____

G2: _____

G3: _____

   a. What is the position of each of these groups on your legislation?

G1: _____

G2: _____

G3: _____

   b. What kinds of contacts have you had with each of them regarding this legislation?

	G1	G2	G3
mail	_____	_____	_____
telephone	_____	_____	_____
office call	_____	_____	_____

lunch _____ _____ _____

parties _____ _____ _____

committee testimony _____ _____ _____

other (specify) _____ _____ _____

_____ _____ _____ _____

_____ _____ _____ _____

_____ _____ _____ _____

   c. How frequent were your contacts with representatives of these groups? (try to get time period)

G1: _____

G2: _____

G3: _____

   d. Who made the initial contacts, your office or theirs?

G1: _____

G2: _____

G3: _____

   e. Do you know how much contact your staff has had with each of these groups?

G1: _____

G2: _____

G3: _____

  4. From your position, how important a part would you say these groups played in the progress of the bill thus far? (allow commentary **before** asking for a ranking)

G1: _____

G2: _____

G3. _____

	G1	G2	G3
extremely important	____	____	____
moderately important	____	____	____
not very important	____	____	____
unimportant	____	____	____

  5. When you were working on the bill, what was your personal

reaction to what these groups were doing? (allow commentary **before** asking check list)

G1: _____

G2: _____

G3: _____

	G1	G2	G3
Informative	____	____	____
Co-operative	____	____	____
Unco-operative	____	____	____
Irritating	____	____	____
Irrelevant	____	____	____
Uninformed	____	____	____

Other (specify)

_____ ____ ____ ____

_____ ____ ____ ____

_____ ____ ____ ____

6. Did you feel noticeably "pushed" or "pressured" by these groups?

G1: _____

G2: _____

G3: _____

How did you feel about their actions? _____

7. Did you feel that their activities significantly limited your own choices of action?

G1: _____

G2: _____

G3: _____

8. When the committee went over (marked up) the bill in executive session, do you think particular members of the committee paid much attention to the views of these interest groups? Which of these groups seemed to be the most effective?

G1: _____

G2: _____

G3: _____

     (own reference) member of committee: yes_____ no_____

I realize that no one has time to work actively on all of the bills that come up in Congress each session. Each person can only be informed and active on a small number of bills. Therefore, I would like to get your reactions to organized interest group activity on a bill that you have **not** made your special concern.

    9. Have you worked on any of the following bills this session?
      (choose one from card on which respondent has **not** worked)

  10. On _____bill, what contacts have you personally had with organized interest groups?_____
      What were the names of some of these groups? _____

_____

_____

    a. What position did each of these groups take on this bill?
G1: _____
G2: _____
G3: _____
Other: _____

    b. What kinds of contact have you had with each of these groups regarding this legislation?

	G1	G2	G3	Other
mail	____	____	____	____
telephone	____	____	____	____
office call	____	____	____	____
lunch	____	____	____	____
social gathering	____	____	____	____
committee testimony	____	____	____	____
other (specify)				
_____	____	____	____	____
_____	____	____	____	____
_____	____	____	____	____

c. How frequent were your contacts with representatives of these groups? (try to get time period)

G1: _____

G2: _____

G3: _____

Other: _____

d. Who made the initial contacts, your office or theirs?

G1: _____

G2: _____

G3: _____

Other: _____

e. Do you know how much contact members of your staff may have had with each of these groups?

G1: _____

G2: _____

G3: _____

Other: _____

11. From your position, how important a part would you say these groups played in the progress of the bill thus far? (allow commentary **before** asking for a ranking)

G1: _____

G2: _____

G3: _____

Other: _____

	G1	G2	G3	Other
extremely important	___	___	___	___
moderately important	___	___	___	___
not very important	___	___	___	___
unimportant	___	___	___	___

12. What was your personal reaction to what these groups were doing? (allow commentary **before** asking the check list)

G1: _____

G2: _____

G3: _____

Other: _____

	G1	G2	G3	Other
Informative	____	____	____	____
Co-operative	____	____	____	____
Unco-operative	____	____	____	____
Irritating	____	____	____	____
Irrelevant	____	____	____	____
Uninformed	____	____	____	____
Other (specify)				
____	____	____	____	____
____	____	____	____	____
____	____	____	____	____

(check as many as necessary)

13. Did you feel noticeably "pushed" or "pressured" at any time by these groups?

G1: _____

G2: _____

G3: _____

Other: _____

How did you feel about their actions?_____

14. Did you feel that their activities significantly limited your own choices of action?

G1: _____

G2: _____

G3: _____

Other: _____

We have been talking about your personal experience with organized interest groups on specific issues. I would like to ask you a few questions on your general reaction and attitudes towards organized interest group activities.

15. Just how important do you think organized interest groups—

either organized lobbies or constituency groups—are in getting Congressional action that is favorable to them? _____

16. In general, what techniques that these groups may use would be most effective? (allow commentary **before** asking check list)

letters _____

petitions _____

telegrams _____

telephone _____

office call _____

social engagement _____

committee testimony _____

contact through personal friend _____

campaign work _____

campaign contribution _____

invitation to meetings _____

casual conversation with constituent _____

other (specify)

_____ _____

_____ _____

_____ _____

_____ _____

17. Many of the writers on Congress, both political scientists and journalists, put a great deal of emphasis on the part played by interest groups in getting favorable Congressional action. It is my idea that while these groups play a role, the extent of interest group influence is often greatly exaggerated and, therefore, the actual workings of the House are seriously misunderstood. Would you care to comment on this? _____